THE UNIVERSITY OF MICHIGAN
CENTER FOR CHINESE STUDIES

MICHIGAN PAPERS IN CHINESE STUDIES
NO. 31

ECONOMIC TRENDS IN THE REPUBLIC OF CHINA, 1912-1949

by
Albert Feuerwerker

Ann Arbor

Center for Chinese Studies
The University of Michigan

1977

ISBN 0-89264-031-6

Printed in the United States of America

PREFACE

This monograph is an extensive revision
and enlargement of an earlier essay published under the title The Chinese Economy, 1912-1949 as No. 1 of the Michigan
Papers in Chinese Studies. I am greatly
indebted to Professor Thomas G. Rawski
for his many suggestions for improving
my effort to summarize the condition of
China's pre-1949 economy.

20 April 1977
Ann Arbor

CONTENTS

LIST OF TABLES

1. Introduction

To survey the history of the Chinese economy from the end of the Manchu dynasty to the establishment of the People's Republic is inevitably to tell a tale in a minor key. The years before 1949 saw no "take-off" toward sustained growth of aggregate output and the possibility of increased individual welfare which might accompany it. At best, in welfare terms, the great majority of the Chinese merely sustained and reproduced themselves at the subsistence level to which, the callous might say, they had long since become accustomed. In the bitter decade of war and civil war which began in the mid-1930s, the standard of life for many fell short even of that customary level.[1]

A cautious weighing of what little is definitely known suggests that aggregate output grew only slowly during 1912-1949, and that there was no increase in per capita income. Nor was there any downward trend in average income. Although a small modern industrial and transportation sector, which first appeared in the late nineteenth century, continued to grow at a comparatively rapid rate, its impact was still a minor one before 1949. The relative factor supply of land, labor, and capital remained basically unaltered. The occupational distribution of the population was not much changed; nor in spite of some expansion of the urban population was the urban-rural ratio significantly disturbed during these four decades. While some new products were introduced from abroad and from domestic factories, quantitatively they were a mere dribble and affected the quality of life hardly at all. Institutions for the creation of credit remained few and feeble; the organization of a unified national market was never achieved. Foreign trade was relatively unimportant to the bulk of the population. Throughout rural China a demographic pattern of high birthrates and high death rates persisted. Economic hardship, in rural China in particular, was endemic and probably grew more critical after the outbreak of war in 1937. Yet in the absence of

1

a profound transformation of values in a significant portion of the elite leadership of Chinese society, which led ultimately to the harnessing of this distress to political ends not directly determined by the processes of the economy itself, there is no good reason to believe that the economic system would have either collapsed catastrophically or advanced rapidly toward modern economic growth. As a system, China's economy which was "premodern" even in the mid-twentieth century ceased to be viable only after 1949--and then as a consequence of explicit political choice by the victorious Communist Party and not primarily as a result of lethal economic contradictions.

While the quantitative indicators do not show large changes during the republican era, China in 1949 was nevertheless different than China in 1912. The small industrial and transportation sector and, perhaps even more, the reservoir of technical skills and of experience with complex economic organizations--the hundreds of thousands of workers, technicians, and managers who had themselves "become modern"--provided a base upon which the People's Republic of China could and did build.

As a crude first approximation, the Chinese economy prior to 1949 may be described as consisting of a large agricultural (or rural) sector encompassing approximately 75 percent of the population and a much smaller nonagricultural (or urban) sector with its principal base in the semimodern treaty port cities. Rural China grew the agricultural products which constituted 65 percent of national output, but also engaged the handicrafts, petty trade, and old-fashioned transportation. To the urban sector was attached, with ties of varying strength, an agricultural hinterland located mainly along rivers and railways leading to the ports. This hinterland may be differentiated from the bulk of rural China by the greater degree to which it sold to and bought from the coastal and riverine cities of the urban sector.

The agricultural sector was composed mainly of sixty to seventy million family farms--perhaps one-half owner-operated, one-quarter farmed by part-owners who rented varying portions of their land, and the remaining quarter cultivated by tenant farmers--whose members lived in the several hundred thousand villages which filled most of the landscape of the arable parts of China. In the course of the first half of the twentieth century, the average size of these farms decreased as the growth of population exceeded increments to arable land. Only a few areas in rural China (in the regions of dense population) lacked agglomerated settlements--parts of Szechwan, for example, where scattered farmsteads were the norm. The typical landscape was dotted with clusters of houses arranged along one or more streets which were surrounded by the village fields. So closely spaced were the villages in the areas of densest settlement that one was often within sight of another. Where, in response to local disorder which grew in the nineteenth century, villages first in north China and then also in the south had erected protective walls around the houses and other structures in the village center, the village was defined by the inhabitants living within its earthen or brick ramparts. This definition was supported by the circumstance that many villages were made up of populations who possessed the same or a small number of different surnames which corresponded to the lineage or lineages to which the inhabitants belonged. The boundaries between the fields belonging to the residents of one village and those owned by its closest neighbors were not, however, so unambiguously distinguishable. In the course of time farmland changed hands, and it was not unusual that the mortgagee (and possible eventual owner) of property in village A should be a resident of village B, or even of village X at some distance removed from A.

This indeterminacy of village boundaries began to change only in the last part of the nineteenth century when increased tax demands by hsien governments made it essential that the villages be concerned about the precise areas in which the new levies would be collected. Even in the twentieth century, while more formal village organizations were elaborated, the rural village was usually not an effective political unit—certainly not for the purpose of organizing its human and material resources for economic development. Indeed, the frequent inability of higher levels of government before 1949 to penetrate into the basic "natural" units of Chinese society except to collect taxes was one factor underlying the perpetuation of China's traditional economy into the middle of the twentieth century.

While household and village were natural social units and not imposed by the state as the revived pao-chia (registration and police) system was from the 1920s onward, the peasant's horizon was not bounded by them. The normal limits of person-to-person social interaction were not the village boundaries, but rather the borders of a higher order community composed of several (a dozen or more) villages and the market town which served them. A high proportion of China's farm households produced all or much of their own food. Grains, cash crops, and local agricultural specialties, as well as the products of household handicraft (perhaps 30 percent by value of farm output), were, however, regularly marketed. The peasant sector may in fact also be described as consisting of a large number of local markets roughly defined by a radius equal to the distance which a peasant buyer or seller and his products might cover on foot in one day. These markets were normally periodic rather than continuous, convening every few days according to one of several scheduling systems which were characteristic of different regions of China. Skinner, who refers to these basic units as "standard marketing areas" (SMA), has suggested that "the rural countryside of late traditional China can be viewed as a grid of approximately 70,000 hexagonal cells, each an economic system focused on a standard market."[2] The bulk of the trading in standard markets consisted of a horizontal exchange of goods among peasants. To some extent there was an upward flow out of the SMA of handicraft items and local agricultural specialties; the principal outflow of staples, however, consisted of tax grains to the government level of the economy. Increasingly in the late-nineteenth and twentieth centuries the SMA was the ultimate destination of new commodities either manufactured in the treaty ports or imported from abroad.

To the limited extent that rural China began to produce staples for export, including technical crops for the treaty port factories, these tended to move in new commercial channels alternative to the traditional periodic markets. In the agricultural hinterland of the east coast treaty ports, in particular, a modern town economy developed alongside of the periodic-marketing economy. But in the vast bulk of rural China the traditional market structure was flourishing with few signs of decay right down to 1949, a strong indication that the rural economy had not been substantially transformed. The peasant household in the mid-twentieth century probably depended more on commodities not produced by itself or its neighbors than was the case fifty years earlier. But because there was little real improvement in transportation at the local level, the primary marketing area was not enlarged so as to bring about a radical replacement of standard markets by modern commercial channels organized around larger regional marketing complexes.

Nonagricultural, or "urban," does not necessarily imply "modern." At the beginning of the nineteenth century, perhaps as many as 12 million persons (3 to 4 percent of the then 350 million Chinese) lived in cities with populations of thirty thousand or more. With few exceptions, these cities were primarily administrative centers--the national capital, Peking, with nearly one million inhabitants; major provincial capitals; and the largest prefectural (fu) cities. Some were simultaneously important centers of interprovincial and interregional commerce: Nanking, Soochow, Hankow, Canton, Foochow, Hangchow, Chungking, Chengtu, and Sian. These cities were the loci of the highest officials of the empire, the major military garrisons, the wealthiest merchant groups, and the most skilled artisans. Their populations included, too, prominent nonofficial gentry, lesser merchants, the numerous underlings who staffed the government yamens, laborers and transport workers, as well as the little-studied literate stratum of monks, priests, jobless lower-degree holders, failed examination candidates, demobilized military officers, and the like who were part of the "transients, migrants, and outsiders"[3] so prominent in the traditional Chinese city. But the patterns of late-Ch'ing city life, political and economic, greatly resembled what they had been in the Sung dynasty five centuries earlier.

From the mid-nineteenth century onward, as a consequence of the establishment of a foreign presence in China, the Chinese city began to add modern economic, political, and cultural roles to the phenomena which continued from late-traditional times. The total number of urban residents grew slowly in the course of the nineteenth century, at a rate not much greater than total population growth; and then more rapidly between 1900 and 1938, at almost twice the average population growth rate. Cities with populations over fifty thousand in 1938 included approximately 27.3 million inhabitants, 5 to 6 percent of a total population of 500 million. These same cities had perhaps 16.8 million inhabitants at the turn of the century, 4 to 5 percent of a 430 million population. The difference suggests an annual growth rate for all large cities of about 1.4 percent. China's six largest cities--Shanghai, Peking, Tientsin, Canton, Nanking, and Hankow--however, were growing at rates of 2 to 7 percent per annum in the 1930s.[4]

Ninety-two cities had been formally opened to foreign trade by World War I, and while some of these "treaty ports" were in fact places of minor importance, a high proportion of China's largest cities were among them (some important exceptions: Sian, K'aifeng, Peking, Taiyuan, Wuhsi, Shaoshing, Nanch'ang, Chengtu). The treaty ports were the termini of the railroad lines which began to appear in the 1890s and of the steam shipping which spread along China's coast and on the Yangtze and West rivers. Foreign commercial firms opened branches and agencies in the larger treaty ports, and under the provisions of the Treaty of Shimonoseki of April 1895, foreigners were permitted to organize manufacturing operations in them (some had done so illegally before 1896). Chinese firms specializing in foreign trade and its adjuncts made their appearances parallel to the arrival of the foreigner. While not restricted to the open ports, most of the small but growing Chinese-owned industrial sector which began to appear in the 1870s was also located in these same cities. In the shadow of the modern factories, Chinese and foreign, handicraft workshops flourished either as sub-contractors or, as in the case of cotton weaving, as major customers for the output of the new spinning mills. The processing of exports, still largely a handicraft operation, also burgeoned in the major port cities. For a small number of urban dwellers, in addition to manufac-turing and commerce, a number of new occupations in the free profes-sions, in journalism and publishing, and in modern educational and cultural institutions gradually came into being.

But this modern industrial, commercial, and transportation sector remained confined for the most part to the treaty ports. Only to a very limited degree did it replace traditional handicrafts, existing marketing systems, or transportation by human and animal backs, carts, sampans, and junks. There was almost no spillover into the agricultural sector, for example, in the form of improved technology (new seeds, chemical fertilizer, modern water control, farm machinery) or more efficient organization (credit, stable marketing, rationalized land use).[5] The fluctuations of world markets for silver or for China's agricultural exports, experienced directly first in the treaty ports, could at times send ripples of influence into the countryside. Overall, however, the peasant sector and the treaty port economy remained only very loosely linked until 1949.

II. Economic Statistics

National economic statistics that are either comprehensive or reliable are a regrettable lacuna even for twentieth-century China. The Ministry of Agriculture and Commerce of the Peking government did publish a series of annual statistical tables;[6] statistical reports were issued, for example, by the national railroads;[7] and, of course, the generally excellent foreign trade statistics of the foreign-adminis-tered Chinese Maritime Customs appeared annually.[8] For the most part, however, the central government before 1928 was so weak and ineffectual that no systematic national effort was made to collect eco-nomic data.

With the establishment of the Kuomintang government, the statis-tical situation improved somewhat. The Annual Reports of the Ministry of Finance for the years 1928-1934 are the only genuine reports on Chinese national finance ever issued.[9] For the 1930s, agricultural statistics, including acreage and crop production, were compiled by the National Agricultural Research Bureau of the Ministry of Industries and made available in its monthly publication Nung-ch'ing pao-kao [Crop reports, 1933-1939]. These estimates, together with the privately sponsored work of J. L. Buck covering the late 1920s and early 1930s at the College of Agriculture, University of Nanking, are about the best data available on Chinese agriculture. [10] The only year for which we have detailed industrial statistics is 1933. These are the products of a large-scale survey made by D. K. Lieu for the National Resources Commission of the National Military Council [11] Lieu's data, however, exclude both Manchuria and foreign-owned factories in China outside of Manchuria, although Japanese studies of Manchurian industry are available. [12] There are also a number of estimates of foreign-owned industry in China, but none of them are comparable to Lieu's survey. In addition to government-sponsored collections of statistics, good but fragmentary private collections of data were carried out by the Nankai Institute of Economics in Tientsin (mainly price data)[13] and in Shanghai by the China Institute of Economic and Statistical Research. [14]

Although in quantity and quality they were much superior to pre-1928 data, the economic statistics of the Kuomintang period still left much to be desired, in part because China was still far from being politically unified; in part because a large proportion of economic activity continued to be carried on outside of any market transactions and thus could not easily be measured; and finally because of the continued technical backwardness of the statistical services. But even the relatively deficient data of 1928-1937 are a godsend when compared to what is available thereafter. War and civil war did not spare statistical collection any more than other parts of the administrative organization. For 1937-1949, macrodata of any kind, apart from fiscal and monetary statistics, are scarce and unreliable. [15]

The statistical publications that I have noted are, of course, only examples. There were more--the publications of the Ministry of Industry and the Bureau of Foreign Trade of the Nanking government, for instance, or the rural surveys prepared for the Executive Yuan's Rural Recovery Commission as well as the comprehensive mineral output data for China proper and Manchuria published by the Geological Survey of China. In addition to these official reports, Chinese and Japanese researchers (the latter mainly on behalf of the South Manchurian Railway Company) produced hundreds of fragmentary local studies. But none of these individually--nor all of them collectively--supply or easily permit the derivation of the comprehensive data on population, employment, capital stock, national product and expenditure, prices, taxation, monetary flows, and the like which the economic historian might use for a definitive analysis of China's economy in the first half of the twentieth century.[16]

It is under these handicaps that the Chinese economy in the period of the republic must be surveyed. That so much of the macroeconomic description included in this monograph hangs on what are, after all, only intelligent guesses for 1933 makes it admittedly a hostage to fortune. Chinese domestic materials, inadequate as they are, have not yet been fully exploited, and careful use of studies of the twentieth-century Chinese economy by such Japanese agencies as the South Manchurian Railway will probably show that they contributed more than I have seemed to credit them. Caveat lector.

III. Population

A point of diminishing returns has probably been reached in the manipulation of available Chinese population statistics. The census-registration of 1953-1954 which reported a population of 583 million for mainland China is, on the balance of the evidence, the nearest to an accurate count of the population of China that has ever been made. This large number is at odds with such estimates as the Kuomintang official figure of 463, 493, 000 for 1948; but the latter and several dozen more official and private estimates have all been more in the nature of guesses than the 1953-1954 census, whatever its technical shortcomings.[17] A population of approximately 580 million in 1953 fits quite well a putative average increase of 0. 8 percent per year between 1912 and 1953, such a rate as might be expected from a demographic situation of slow but irregular growth resulting from the difference between high and fluctuating death rates and high but relatively stable birth-rates. While no statistical data are available, it appears likely that population growth was sufficiently greater than this average during the Yuan Shih-k'ai presidency (1912-1916), the Nanking government decade (1928-1937), and the first years of the People's Republic (1950-1958) to compensate for the probable negative demographic effects of the war-lord period and the war and civil war of 1937-1949. Starting with approximately 430 million persons in 1912, the population of mainland China in 1933 was some 500 million and grew to about 580 million in 1953.

Liu and Yeh have made detailed estimates of the occupational distribution of the total population for 1933. Judging from more fragmentary data for individual provinces or cities for the previous two decades, this distribution was largely unchanged during the republican period. Table 1 summarizes the Liu-Yeh estimates.

Of a total working population in 1933 of 259.21 million, 204.91 million or 79 percent actually engaged in farming and 54.3 million (including man-labor units apportioned from joint occupations) or 21 percent followed nonagricultural pursuits. Seventy-three percent of the total population lived in families having agriculture as their main occupation, while 27 percent were members of nonagricultural families. Although twentieth-century China experienced some industrial growth in the treaty ports and some development of mining and railroad transportation, the small numbers engaged in these occupations even in 1933 suggests that the occupational distribution of China's population as a whole had changed little from what it had been at the end of the Ch'ing dynasty. By way of contrast, it might be noted that in the United States only 21.4 percent of those aged ten years or more and gainfully occupied were engaged in agriculture in 1930. To find figures even remotely comparable to those of China in 1933, one would need to look at America in 1820 or 1830 when 70 percent of the labor force worked in agriculture.

IV. National Income

Two major independent estimates of China's national income in the republican period have been made, one by Liu Ta-chung and Yeh Kung-chia and the other by Ou Pao-san (Wu Pao-san) (see table 2). The aggregates differ widely--the larger estimate is about 40 percent greater than the smaller--but the only important difference between the two is value added in agriculture. Both estimates are for the year 1933 only.

The Liu-Yeh data--probably the more reliable of the two--may be summarized as follows: agriculture of course bulked greatest in the 1933 net domestic product, contributing 65 percent in 1933 prices. All "industry" (factories, handicrafts, mining, utilities) contributed 10.5 percent. Trade was third with 9.4 percent. Other sectors ranked as follows: transportation, 5.6 percent; finance, personal service, and rent, 5.6 percent; government administration, 2.8 percent; and construction, 1.2 percent. Another way of stating the composition of national income in 1933 is to note that the modern nonagricultural sectors (very generously defined as factories, mining, utilities, construction, modern trade and transportation, trading stores, restaurants, and

TABLE 1

OCCUPATIONAL DISTRIBUTION, 1933

	Millions	Percentage of 500 Million
Total population	500.00	100.00
Agricultural population	365.00	73.00
Working population, ages 7-64	212.30	42.46
Agriculture only	118.78	23.76
Joint agriculture and subsidiary occupations [a]	93.52	18.70
Agriculture	86.13	17.23
Industry [b]	3.61	0.72
Trade	1.66	0.33
Transportation	1.14	0.23
Other nonagricultural occupations [c]	0.98	0.20
Children under 7	71.21	14.24
Students, age 7 and over	5.13	1.02
Age 65 and over	10.99	2.20
Unemployed or idle, ages 7-64 [d]	65.36	13.07
Nonagricultural population	135.00	27.00
Working population, ages 7-64 [e]	46.91	9.38
Factories	1.13	0.23
Handicrafts	12.13	2.43
Mining	0.77	0.15
Utilities	0.04	0.01

Construction	1.55	0.31
Trade	13.22	2.64
Transportation	10.16	2.03
Other nonagricultural occupations	7.91	1.58
Children		
Under 7	26.33	5.26
Under 12	43.86	8.77
Students		
Age 7 and over	5.74	1.15
Age 12 and over	0.60	0.12
Age 65 and over	4.08	0.82
Unemployed or idle [c]		
Ages 7-64	51.94	10.39
Ages 12-64	39.56	7.91

Source: Ta-chung Liu and Kung-chia Yeh, The Economy of the Chinese Mainland: National Income and Economic Development, 1933-1959 (Princeton: Princeton University Press, 1965), tables 54 and 55, pp. 185, 188.

[a] In the listing below, man-labor units are apportioned to each part of joint occupations.

[b] Manufacturing, home industries, mining, utilities, and construction.

[c] Professional and public service, etc.

[d] Including housewives.

[e] Actual age of the working nonagricultural population falls mostly within the range 12-64; age 7 is taken as the lower limit merely for the convenience of grouping on the same basis as the agricultural working population.

TABLE 2

DOMESTIC PRODUCT, 1933
(Billion 1933 Chinese $)

Net Value Added in:	Liu-Yeh		Ou
Agriculture	18.76		12.59
Factories	0.64		0.38
Producers' goods		0.16	
Consumers' goods		0.47	
Handicrafts	2.04		1.36
Identified portion		1.24	
Others		0.80	
Mining	0.21		0.24
Utilities	0.13		0.15
Construction	0.34		0.22
Transportation and communications	1.63		0.92
Modern		0.43	
Old-fashioned		1.20	
Trade	2.71		2.54
Trading stores and restaurants		1.75	
Peddlers		0.96	
Government administration	0.82		0.64
Finance	0.21		0.20
Personal services	0.34		0.31
Residential rents	1.03		0.93
(Less double counting of banking services)			(−0.17)
Net domestic product	28.86		20.32
Depreciation	1.02		1.45
Gross domestic product	29.88		21.77

Sources: Ou Pao-san's 1948 Harvard Ph.D. thesis, "Capital Formation and
Consumers' Outlay in China," pp. 204-211, summarizes the data in his
Chung-kuo kuo-min so-te, i-chiu-san-san-nien [China's national income,
1933], 2 vols., (Shanghai: Chung-hua, 1947) and takes account of his later
revisions. Ta-chung Liu and Kung-chia Yeh, The Economy of the Chinese Mainland, table 8, p. 66.

modern financial institutions) contributed only 12.6 percent of the total. Agriculture, traditional nonagricultural sectors (handicrafts, old-fashioned transportation, peddlers, traditional financial institutions, personal services, rent), and government administration accounted for 87.4 percent. The structure of China's mainland economy before 1949 was typical of a pre-industrial society when looked at from the expenditure side as well. By end use, 91 percent of gross domestic expenditure in 1933 went to personal consumption. Communal services and government consumption together accounted for 4 percent, while gross investment totalled 5 percent.

To what degree 1933, a depression year, may be characteristic of the entire republican period is perhaps questionable, but no comparably complete national income estimates for any other year have been attempted. Perkins, however, has converted the Liu-Yeh data into 1957 prices, substituted his own somewhat lower farm output figures, [18] and added estimates for 1914-1918 with results that suggest a slowly growing gross domestic product during the republican era, one which was also changing slightly in composition (see table 3).

The absolute values shown in tables 2 and 3 are not comparable because one is stated in 1933 prices and the other in 1957 prices. Additionally, the 1914-1918 figures are constructed from plausible guesses as well as true estimates. But the overwhelming predominance of the traditional sectors up to 1949 and the quantitatively small but qualitatively significant changes over four decades which these tables imply fit very well with other information, presented in the remaining sections of this monograph, concerning the separate sectors of the Chinese economy during the republic. [19] Modern manufacturing and mining grew steadily from modest late-nineteenth century beginnings until the outbreak of war with Japan in 1937. In Manchuria, this growth continued and even accelerated during the war. Modern transportation--railroads and steam shipping--experienced a comparable expansion, not replacing traditional communications but supplementing them. A modern financial sector, banking in particular, largely supplanted traditional banking in urban China in the course of the first half of the twentieth century. But even in 1933 Perkins estimates the contribution of the modern sectors (more narrowly defined than in my summary of the Liu-Yeh data in that he excludes modern services) as only 7 percent of gross domestic product, more than twice the 3 percent of 1914-1918 but still minuscule.

The growth of total GDP between 1912 and 1949 therefore came also from increased output by the traditional sectors, mainly agriculture

TABLE 3

GROSS DOMESTIC PRODUCT, 1914-1918, 1933, 1952
(1957 Prices)

Sector	1914-1918		1933		1952	
	Billion 1957 yuan					
Manufacturing+[a]	8.5		11.77		17.23	
Modern [b]		1.3		4.54		11.11
Agriculture	29.9		35.23		31.58	
Services	10.0		12.52		17.07	
Depreciation [c]	---		2.19		---	
GDP	48.4		61.71		65.88	
	Ratio to GDP					
Manufacturing	.176		.198		.262	
Modern		.027		.074		.169
Agriculture	.618		.592		.459	
Services	.207		.210		.259	
GDP	1.000		1.000		1.000	

Source: Dwight H. Perkins, "Growth and Changing Structure of China's Twentieth-Century Economy," in Perkins, ed., China's Modern Economy in Historical Perspective (Stanford: Stanford University Press, 1975), table 1, p. 117.

[a] M[+]=industry (modern and premodern, manufacturing, mining, and utilities) plus transportation.

[b] Modern=factory output, mining, utilities, modern transportation.

[c] Not netted out of the individual sectors except for 1933; distributed among the sectors in proportion to their net products to calculate the ratios in the lower half of the table.

and handicrafts. Agricultural production grew slowly, but with annual
and regional variations due to weather and politico-military circumstances, in the first decades of the twentieth century. The largest
increases occurred in newly developed areas such as Manchuria and
parts of southwestern China. Elsewhere the value of agricultural output was augmented by the increased production of cash crops. Handicraft production has not yet been adequately studied; but for the reasons
which I suggest below in my discussion of industry it is extremely un-
likely that total handicraft output, as opposed to its relative share,
declined between 1912 and 1949. The contrary is a more plausible
conclusion.

If we compare the estimates of gross domestic product in table 3
with population estimates of 430 million in 1912, 500 million in 1933,
and 572 million in 1952, we find that per capita GDP in each of these
years was on the order of (in 1957 prices) 113, 123, and 115 yuan
respectively. Given the potential errors in all of this data, it would
be misleading to make a statement stronger than the following: the
best estimates now available do not show any pronounced upward or
downward trend in per capita GDP in the decades covered by this monograph if one omits the twelve years of war and civil war which began
in 1937.

During the war with Japan and in the last years of the civil war
which brought down the Nationalist government, per capita output and
income in some parts of China probably fell sharply. Some notably
articulate groups--teachers and government employees on fixed salaries
which did not keep up with the inflation, but not urban workers who
fared relatively well after the war and before the final collapse of 1948-
1949--were adversely affected. North China saw a crippling of farm
production and a breakdown of the commercial links between town and
countryside in the wake of the Japanese invasion. During the civil war
of 1946-1949, agricultural and commercial conditions were probably
worse in that region where the fighting was centered than elsewhere in
China. After 1940 crop production began to decline in unoccupied China
and averaged about 9 percent below 1939 for the remainder of the war.
The introduction of a land tax in kind and compulsory grain borrowing
in 1942, together with accelerated military conscription which caused
severe labor shortages, appear to have reduced the real income of
peasants. But industrial production in Kuomintang-controlled areas
in the interior, beginning from a low base, grew until 1942 or 1943. In
the postwar period, the resumption of inflation in 1946 and its runaway
character during 1948-1949 had much more serious consequences in the

coastal, urban sector than in the rural interior of south and west China where total output probably changed little. Nevertheless, flows of food and agricultural raw materials to the cities were curtailed as the value of the currency declined precipitously.[20]

We have little information on the distribution of income in prewar republican China, so that it is at least possible that the income of a significant part of the population was declining while average per capita GDP remained constant or rose slightly. But in the rural areas and among the majority of the farming population "there is no convincing evidence that landlords were garnering an increasing share of the product during the first half of the twentieth century. The limited available data, in fact, suggest that the rate of tenancy might even have declined slightly, and that in periods of political turmoil landlords often had difficulty collecting their rents."[21]

Allegiances were certainly changed during 1937-1949, but even then not primarily because the economy could not support China's population at the prevailing (and low) standard of living in the absence of severe man-made or natural disasters. The rapid recovery which by 1952 had returned output to peak pre-1949 levels was based almost entirely on the success of a new and effective government in restoring the production of existing enterprises, not on new investment. For the rest of the four decades before 1949, civil war in the 1920s and early 1930s, droughts (e.g., in 1920-1921 in north China), floods (e.g., of the Yangtze River in 1931), and other natural disasters indeed undermined the general welfare of the Chinese people, but not necessarily their material welfare, a distinction of substantial importance. Even a slightly rising income is poor compensation for the heightened personal insecurity occasioned by political turmoil and warfare, while on the contrary a low but stable per capita income may be acceptable if offered in a context of greater personal and national security.

V. Industry

In describing the Chinese economy in the closing years of the Ch'ing dynasty, I noted that at least 549 Chinese-owned private and semi-official manufacturing and mining enterprises using mechanical power were inaugurated between 1895 and 1913. The total initial capitalization of these firms was Ch$ 120,288,000.[22] In addition, 96 foreign-owned and 40 Sino-foreign enterprises established in the same period had an initial capitalization of Ch$ 103,153,000. This was of course only a crude estimate, not the findings of an industrial census but a compilation of available information from a variety of contemporary official and nonofficial sources.

Two similar tabulations, which exclude modern mines but include arsenals and utilities, suggest an appreciable expansion of Chinese-owned modern industry during and immediately following World War I. The first records 698 factories with an initial capitalization of Ch$ 330, 824, 000 and 270, 717 workers in 1913, while the second notes 1, 759 factories with an initial capitalization of Ch$ 500, 620, 000 and 557, 622 workers in 1920.[23] Concentration on war production by the European powers and the shipping shortage reduced the flow of exports to China and provided an enhanced opportunity for Chinese-owned industry to expand. While orders for equipment were placed earlier--capital goods still came mainly from abroad--the opening of most new plants had to await the end of the war and the actual arrival of the machinery ordered.

Foreign-owned and Sino-foreign enterprises also increased during the first decade of the republic, but little direct investment occurred during 1914-1918. The largest increments came immediately after World War I when, for example, revisions of the Chinese tariff in 1918 and 1922 raising the import duty on the finer count yarns which Japan had been exporting to China served as an inducement for Japan to open new textile mills in China.

Like both the Chinese- and foreign-owned factories established in the last part of the Ch'ing dynasty, factories (and mines) opened in the second decade of the twentieth century were heavily concentrated in Shanghai and Tientsin, and in other places in Kiangsu, Liaoning, Hopei, Kwangtung, Shantung, and Hupei--that is, mainly in the coastal and Yangtze Valley provinces.[24]

The first and only industrial census in republican China, for the year 1933, was made by investigators of the Institute of Economic and Statistical Research under the direction of D. K. Lieu (Liu Ta-chün). It was based on statistical information gathered directly from factory managers and--apart from its exclusion of all foreign-owned firms, as well as Manchuria, Kansu, Sinkiang, Yunnan, Kweichow, Ninghsia, Tsinghai, Tibet, and Mongolia (none of these except Manchuria had any significant number of modern factories)--is considered to be fairly reliable. Published in 1937, Lieu's survey recorded 2,435 Chinese-owned factories capitalized at Ch$ 406, 926, 634, with a gross output valued at Ch$ 1, 113, 974, 413 and employment of 493, 257 workers.[25]

These factories were concentrated in the coastal provinces, and especially in Shanghai which accounted for 1,186 of the plants surveyed. More than 80 percent of Chinese-owned industry in 1933 was located in the eastern and southeastern coastal provinces and Liaoning in Manchuria; and this proportion would be higher still if foreign-owned establishments, which were limited to the treaty ports, were included in the estimate.

In his study of China's national income in 1933, Ou Pao-san supplemented Lieu's survey by adding estimates for foreign-owned factories in China proper and for factories in Manchuria and the other omitted provinces. His revised estimate reported a total of 3,841 factories (3,167 Chinese-owned and 674 foreign-owned), with a gross output valued at Ch$ 2,186,159,000 (Chinese: $1,415,459,000; foreign: $770,700,000) and employment of 738,029 workers.[26]

Liu Ta-chung and Yeh Kung-chia have more recently provided a further revision of Lieu's survey. Their figures appear to be as good as we shall get given the problems with the underlying data, and I follow them in table 4 which shows the gross value of output and the number of workers in the several branches of China's modern industrial sector in 1933. Manufacturing establishments using mechanical power, regardless of the number of workers in each, in China proper and Manchuria produced a gross output valued at Ch$ 2,645,400,000 in 1933 and employed a total of 1,075,800 workers. Although Liu-Yeh, in contrast to Lieu and Ou, exclude utilities from their estimate, their totals are substantially higher. This results in part from their broader definition of a factory; from better coverage of Manchuria; and from the utilization of sources other than Lieu's survey for their cotton yarn, cotton cloth, cement, pig iron, and steel data.

For the remaining years before 1949, no really comparable data are at hand, in particular none on the total value of output. The Ministry of Economic Affairs of the Nationalist Government reported in 1937 that, as of that year, 3,935 factories (excluding mines but including utilities and arsenals) had registered with that ministry under the Factory Law. They employed 457,063 workers and had a total capitalization of Ch$ 377,938,000.[27] Of the 3,935 plants, 1,235 (31 percent) were located in Shanghai, 2,063 (52 percent) elsewhere in the coastal provinces, and 637 (17 percent) in the interior. Textiles and food products accounted for 55 percent of the total capitalization of the registered factories. What changes had taken place in the years 1933-1936 during which China experienced some of the effects of the world depression is unclear. The

sizable wartime damage, the fall in production, and the stagnation of
new investment under Japanese occupation in such manufacturing centers
as Shanghai, Tientsin, and Wuhan after 1937 may be inferred from local
and partial qualitative evidence. Similarly, the efforts of the Nationalist
government to develop a manufacturing base, a largely war-related industry, in unoccupied China were widely but incompletely reported.

During 1938-1940, 448 "factories" and 12, 182 "technicians" moved
inland to Szechwan, Hunan, Kwangsi, and Shensi along with the retreating
Nationalist government and armies. At the beginning of 1943, the Ministry of Economic Affairs in Chungking issued an industrial report which,
although it lacked output data, gave some indication of wartime developments in unoccupied China. Of the 3, 758 factories with 241, 662 workers
reported, 590 were in existence in 1937, and 3, 168 were established
during 1938-1942. Their total capitalization, allowing for a tenfold
increase in the index of prices, was approximately equal to that of Shanghai's Chinese-owned industries in 1933; and the number of workers was
also about the same. The bulk of these factories was located in Szechwan
(1, 654), Hunan (501), Shensi (385), and Kwangsi (292), but others were
widely dispersed throughout Kuomintang-controlled areas. In contrast
to the consumers' goods orientation of prewar industry, about 50 percent
(as measured by capitalization) of the new wartime industry produced
military-related and producers' goods. Another contrast with prewar
industry, and one which would continue to be important in the postwar
years, was the major role of state-owned enterprises in this wartime
industrialization. While only 656 (17 percent) of the factories recorded
were "public enterprises" (kung-ying), they represented 69 percent of
the total capitalization, were larger and employed more mechanical
power than privately-owned factories, and dominated the producers'
goods sector (especially chemicals, metals, and machinery).[28]

In table 5, the physical quantities (not values) of output of selected
products in unoccupied China during 1938-1945 are compared with 1933
and 1946 production by Chinese-owned firms in all of China in the form
of index numbers. The pattern of wartime industrialization in Nationalist
areas described above, in particular the emphasis on military-related
producers' goods such as chemicals, is apparent from the table. After
1942, industrial activity in the interior began to slow down, the number
of new firms declined sharply, and output not only ceased to rise but
actually declined in certain capital goods lines. The principal reasons,
apart from raw material shortages and inadequate transport, were
uncertainty about the postwar fate of these inland industries--everyone
was poised to return to Shanghai--and above all inflation. Hoarding

TABLE 4

OUTPUT AND EMPLOYMENT IN MODERN INDUSTRY, 1933

| | Gross Value of Output (Million 1933 Chinese $) | | | | Number of Workers (1,000) | | | |
| | China Proper | | Manchuria | Total | China Proper | | Manchuria | Total |
	Chinese-owned	Foreign-owned			Chinese-owned	Foreign-owned		
Producers' Goods:								
Lumber	4.4	5.6	11.6	21.6	1.2	1.5	2.3	5.0
Machinery, including transportation equipment	55.4	9.9	27.2	92.5	45.7	5.2	14.4	65.3
Ferrous metals and metal products	29.4	1.4	18.1	48.9	15.5	0.4	11.8	27.7
Small electrical appliances	1.3	0.8	---	2.1	0.7	0.3	---	1.0
Stone, clay, and glass products	44.5	1.6	9.7	55.8	34.7	1.1	8.9	44.7
Chemicals and chemical products	58.5	10.0	19.1	87.6	5.6	2.4	4.2	12.2
Textile products	15.3	---	1.6	16.9	4.3	---	0.4	4.7
Leather	37.0	8.1	1.0	46.1	4.5	0.9	0.7	6.1
Paper, paper products, printing	72.0	10.7	3.4	86.1	42.0	3.6	0.8	46.4
Metal coins	41.0	---	---	41.0	0.2	---	---	0.2
Total producers' goods	358.8	48.1	91.7	498.5	154.4	15.4	43.5	213.3

Consumers' Goods:

Wood products	1.2	0.5	0.9	2.6	0.5	0.2	0.8	1.5
Metal products	12.6	1.4	1.6	15.6	4.4	0.5	0.7	5.6
Small electrical appliances	11.9	7.2	0.1	19.2	5.9	2.7	a	8.6
Chinaware and pottery	1.3	0.2	0.7	2.2	1.3	---	1.9	3.2
Chemicals and chemical products	65.3	17.2	4.4	86.9	38.4	7.3	4.9	50.6
Textile products	605.4	257.8	70.6	933.8	380.1	104.7	38.8	523.6
Clothing and attire	101.1	4.6	3.4	109.1	101.7	2.0	3.5	107.2
Leather and rubber products	36.2	2.2	---	38.4	15.1	0.7	---	15.8
Food products	436.3	39.1	158.7	634.1	51.2	8.6	21.6	81.4
Tobacco products, wine, liquor	124.9	117.3	36.0	278.2	20.3	19.0	8.4	47.7
Paper products	2.9	0.5	7.9	11.3	1.8	0.2	4.7	6.7
Miscellaneous	13.5	1.3	0.7	15.5	8.1	1.8	0.7	10.6
Total consumers' goods	1,412.6	449.3	258.0	2,416.9	628.8	147.7	86.0	862.5
Total	1,771.4	497.4	376.7	2,645.4	783.2	163.1	129.5	1,075.8

Source: Liu and Yeh, The Economy of the Chinese Mainland, pp. 142–143, 426–428.

a Less than 100 workers.

TABLE 5

RELATIVE QUANTITIES OF OUTPUT OF SELECTED INDUSTRIAL PRODUCTS, ELECTRIC POWER,
AND COAL IN KUOMINTANG-CONTROLLED AREAS, 1933, 1938–1946

(1933 = 100)

	1933	1938	1939	1940	1941	1942	1943	1944	1945	1946
Coal	100	47	55	57	60	63	66	55	52	182
Pig iron	100	153	182	130	184	278	203	116	140	90
Steel	100	3	4	5	7	10	23	45	61	52
Electric power	100	14	17	21	24	26	27	29	37	683
Cement	100	5	11	11	6	9	8	9	9	65
Alkalies	100	1	1	2	3	3	5	9	5	93
Sulphuric acid	100	3	2	8	10	13	12	15	5	138
Hydrochloric acid	100	8	6	12	10	32	29	32	26	233
Alcohol	100	90	241	1,362	1,605	2,340	2,289	2,180	4,814	3,673
Gasoline	100	--	1	12	35	316	537	675	718	842
Cotton yarn	100	1	2	2	7	7	7	7	4	95
Flour	100	2	3	5	7	7	6	4	3	117

Source: Yen Chung-p'ing, Chung-kuo chin-tai ching-chi shih t'ung-chi tzu-liao hsuan-chi [Selected
statistics on China's modern economic history] (Peking: K'o-hsüeh, 1955), pp. 100–101.

Note: The geographic coverage differs significantly between 1933 and 1946, on the one hand, and the
intervening years on the other. It also differs somewhat from year to year 1938–1945.

and speculation in commodities became more profitable than manufacturing.

Industrial output in occupied China proper probably stagnated or declined during 1937-1945. The evidence is mixed. There was apparently a general fall in production during 1937-1939. In north China, from 1939 or 1940 to 1943 or 1944, the output of coal, iron and steel, cement, electric power, and chemicals showed an increase; but such consumers' goods industries as cotton and wool textiles and flour remained substantially below prewar levels.[29] After a sharp decline, the index of the gross value of factory output (in 1939 prices) in north China had returned to the 1933 level by 1942.[30] Shanghai cotton mills, China's most important industrial plants, however, fared badly during the war. Both yarn and cloth output in Chinese-owned mills fell sharply from 1937, recovered slightly in 1939-1941, and then nearly expired. It is still uncertain whether or not Japanese-controlled firms did any better.

Meanwhile, Manchurian industry under Japanese domination grew rapidly from 1936 to at least 1941. Prior to the mid-1930s, Manchuria's economic growth was based mainly on the extension of the agricultural frontier. Small-scale Chinese-owned factories were in evidence, but the principal modern industries were a network of Japanese-controlled producers' goods enterprises intended to furnish raw and semifinished materials to the Japanese economy. The Anshan and Pen-ch'i ironworks and the Fushun coal mines, large vertically integrated installations, were the most prominent among these units. Subsequent to the consolidation of the Manchukuo puppet state, Japanese interests sponsored a major effort to establish an integrated producers' goods sector. The rate of gross investment in fixed capital, financed largely by capital imports from Japan, which had been 9 percent in 1924, reached 17 percent in 1934 and 23 percent in 1939. (The corresponding rate for China as a whole in 1933 was 5 percent, a figure probably not exceeded before 1949.) Industry broadly defined (mining, manufacturing, public utilities, small-scale industry, and construction) expanded at a rate of 9.9 percent a year between 1936 and 1941 compared to 4.4 percent in the period 1924-1936. Factory industry grew even more rapidly, with the result that Manchuria, with 8 to 9 percent of China's population, contributed almost a third of the total pre-1949 peak Chinese factory product. The rapid development of manufacturing came apparently at the expense of small-scale industry; that is, it was accompanied by a "modernization" of the industrial sector which as a whole expanded at the same rate as the Manchurian gross domestic product and did not gain in relative importance. This appears to be an important contrast with China proper

which I shall note further below. After 1941, as a consequence of the
dwindling flow of equipment, financing, and some critical raw materials
from Japan, both the growth and the diversification of Manchurian industry ground to a halt. Heavy wartime damage and the removal of the
most modern plants and equipment by the Soviet armies in 1945-1946
(losses amounting to one billion U.S. dollars or more) seriously reduced the industrial capacity in Manchuria available to postwar China. [31]

The postwar years 1946-1949 were chaotic and soon dominated by
spreading civil war and rampant inflation. Little useful information
about industrial output is available. Consumers' goods output had probably returned to prewar levels by 1947, but the combination of crippled
productive capacity in Manchurian heavy industry and mining and the
virtual abandonment of the "hothouse" producers' goods factories of the
wartime interior (which had depended on military and other government
orders) after the Nationalist government returned to Nanking resulted
in a substantial decline in the volume of output and the relative importance of this sector. There was briefly, in other words, a return to the
prewar pattern of a heavily consumers' goods oriented industrial structure.

The Japanese surrender was accompanied by a partial breakdown
in industrial output throughout China. In the formerly occupied areas,
Japanese technicians and managers were withdrawn and production came
to a temporary standstill. There was no adequate planning for the takeover of Japanese industry and the restoration of industrial output. The
recovered factories were treated like war booty as each civilian and
military faction struggled to acquire a share of the loot. In the interior,
the plants established during the war were left to wither. The former
Japanese-controlled plants and mines formed the basis for an expanding
state-owned industrial sector. Through the instrumentality of the National Resources Commission, significant parts of producers' goods
output, electric power, and mining came under government control. [32]
At the end of 1947 the Commission managed 291 plants and mines with
a total of 223,770 employees. In the consumers' goods sector, 69 Japanese and "puppet" textile plants (38 cotton mills, 6 woolen mills, 25
related enterprises) were confiscated in 1945 and turned over to a newly
established China Textile Corporation, a joint stock company dominated
by government investment and operated under the direction of the Ministry of Economic Affairs. In 1947, CTC controlled 36.1 percent of the
cotton spindles in China and 59.4 percent of the looms. Its plants produced 43.7 percent of the yarn and 72.6 percent of the cotton cloth.
Supplied with ample working capital by the Chinese government and re-

ceiving preferential treatment in the allocation of foreign exchange for the purchase of raw cotton, the CTC mills had a definite advantage over the private mills--a position analogous to that of the Japanese cotton mills in China whose heirs they were. Except that the Japanese were more efficient. The "carpetbag" managements looked primarily for short-term profits, for themselves and for the KMT government. [33]

At the very end, from late 1948, both government and private factories and mines succumbed to the ravages of runaway inflation, Communist sabotage of transport and the supply of raw materials, power shortages, labor unrest, and human frailty.

Data on some aspects of the history of individual industrial enterprises in republican China are relatively abundant, as, for example, in the collections compiled by Ch'en Chen which are cited frequently above. And the structure of Chinese industry in the 1930s is well known. The critical measure of industrial development, however, is the growth of production over time. John K. Chang's recent construction of an index of industrial production (excluding handicrafts) in mainland China, 1912-1949, which supersedes all previous output estimates, provides a quantitative thread that ties together and confirms the scattered observations offered in the preceding pages. Based on fifteen manufacturing and mining products, covering perhaps 50 percent of industrial output and employing 1933 price weights, Chang's index is presented in table 6. Chinese- and foreign-owned firms, China proper and Manchuria are all included in his estimate. Starting from a very low base, there was a steady rise in industrial production until 1936. Manufacturing and mining as a whole were apparently not adversely affected by the world depression, in spite of the substantial temporary difficulties which contemporary qualitative data report were experienced by many individual factories. Some upward bias is introduced for the depression years by combining China proper and Manchuria, in that Shanghai industry was more severely affected than was industrial enterprise in Manchuria. The outbreak of war brought a sharp decline in 1937-1938, followed by a rise in output in both unoccupied China and Manchuria to a 1942 peak. From 1942 the picture is mixed: a fall in output through 1946, succeeded by a slight recovery in 1947-1948 but not to the 1936 level.

Average annual growth rates for selected subperiods (in net value added) reflect substantial industrial expansion during and after World War I (1912-1920, 13.4 percent) followed by a postwar recession in 1921-1922. From 1923 to 1936, the average rate was 8.7 percent; for 1912-1942, 8.4 percent; and for the whole period 1912-1949--because 1949

TABLE 6

INDEX OF INDUSTRIAL PRODUCTION OF MAINLAND CHINA, 1912-1949
(15 Commodities; 1933 = 100)

Year	Gross Value of Output	Net Value Added
1912	11.9	15.7
1913	15.6	19.2
1914	20.1	24.0
1915	22.5	26.1
1916	24.0	27.7
1917	26.9	32.0
1918	27.8	32.2
1919	34.1	36.9
1920	40.2	42.9
1921	42.4	42.4
1922	34.7	39.0
1923	41.6	45.6
1924	46.9	50.5
1925	55.7	60.1
1926	59.0	61.0
1927	66.6	66.3
1928	72.1	70.5
1929	76.9	75.2
1930	81.6	80.1
1931	88.1	86.5
1932	91.6	90.3
1933	100.0	100.0
1934	103.6	106.8
1935	109.7	119.5
1936	122.0	135.0
1937	96.0	112.3
1938	76.2	104.1
1939	88.2	120.7
1940	94.1	137.6
1941	109.2	161.2
1942	115.7	176.1
1943	105.6	157.1
1944	91.8	140.9
1945	62.0	94.1
1946	90.7	93.6
1947	115.1	116.8
1948	96.7	101.1
1949	105.6	119.2

Source: John K. Chang, Industrial Development in Pre-Communist China: A Quantitative Analysis (Chicago: Aldine, 1939), pp. 60-61.

was a low year--5.6 percent. In a typical prewar year, therefore, the output of China's modern industry and mining as measured in 1933 prices was growing at an impressive rate of 8 to 9 percent. [34]

Yet, as the Liu-Yeh national income estimate in table 2 indicates, industry (including traditional industry) occupied a small place in the Chinese economy; and within the broadly defined industrial sector, modern factory production was overshadowed by handicraft manufacturing. In 1933, the combined output of factories, handicrafts, mining, and utilities in China constituted only 10.5 percent of net domestic product. The output of handicrafts accounted for 67.8 percent of the industrial share; factories, 20.9 percent; mining, 7.0 percent; and utilities, 4.3 percent. Of a total nonagricultural working population estimated at 46.91 million, 12.13 million (25.9 percent) were employed in handicraft industry, 1.13 million (2.4 percent) in factories, 0.77 million (1.6 percent) in mining, and 0.04 million (0.09 percent) in utilities. In spite of the 8 to 9 percent annual rate of growth estimated by Chang, the base from which this growth began was a very low one, with the consequence that the overall sectoral distribution of domestic product was not radically changed during the four decades of the republican era. China's modern industrial sector in the 1930s was small, however, only in relation to contemporary developed economies. As compared, for example, with Japan in 1895 it was neither inconsiderable nor without potential for further development. And in more qualitative terms, the significance of the small modern industrial sector was also far greater than its absolute size might suggest, as I shall indicate below.

There is no doubt that the relative share of handicrafts in the industrial sector as a whole was less in the 1930s than it had been in 1850 or 1912 (see table 3, p. 14). In the mid-nineteenth century, of course, there was no modern industry at all in China, and even in 1912 it was a fragile shoot indeed. Table 7 summarizes the Liu-Yeh estimates of the identified handicraft share in the total output of various industries in 1933. Given the incomplete coverage of handicraft production in the available sources as compared to factory output, the average of 64.5 percent for all industries is certainly too low. [35] Supplementary estimates by Liu and Yeh based on employment and value added per handicraft worker suggest in fact that the handicraft share of gross value added was close to 75 percent in 1933.

Here the relatively hard data end. It has been frequently asserted that traditional handicraft manufacture in the century following the Opium War suffered a continuing decline as a result of competition from both

TABLE 7

HANDICRAFT PRODUCTION AS A PERCENTAGE OF GROSS
VALUE ADDED IN FOURTEEN PRODUCT GROUPS, 1933

Product	Percentage
Lumber and wood products	95.5
Machinery, except electrical	31.3
Metal products	12.1
Electrical appliances	0.5
Transportation equipment	69.4
Stone, clay, and glass products	67.8
Chemical products	22.5
Textile goods	46.1
Clothing and knitted goods	66.5
Leather and allied products	56.2
Food products	90.1
Tobacco, wine, and liquor	30.2
Paper and printing	55.9
Miscellaneous	63.7
All industries	64.5

Source: Liu and Yeh, The Economy of the Chinese Mainland,
  table 38, pp. 142-143 and table G-1, pp. 512-513.

imported foreign goods and the output of Chinese- and foreign-owned modern industry in China.[36] In Manchuria, as indicated above, it may have been the case that factory industry grew at the expense of "small-scale" (i.e., handicraft) industry. But was this equally true of China as a whole? The fragmentary information relating to this matter lends itself better to the conclusion that, in _absolute_ terms, handicraft output as a whole held its own or even increased than it does to the melancholy view just noted.

The matter is complicated by what definition of "handicraft" one uses, the substantially different experiences among handicraft industries, and the point of time at which the several field surveys upon which most commentators rely were taken. Urban or semi-urban handicraft work-shops or "manufactories" (shou-kung-yeh kung-ch'ang) essentially re-moved from the household nexus have been present in the Chinese econ-omy since at least the T'ang dynasty. Their importance, however, as measured both by employment and output, before 1912 at least and to a lesser but unknown extent in the next four decades, was overshadowed by the handicraft production of individual rural and urban households.[37] Thus, for example, it is conceivable that the twentieth-century decline in the absolute output of handspun cotton yarn, which had been primarily a peasant household handicraft, was matched, wholly or in part--the matter awaits study although the data problem is nearly intractable-- by new employment opportunities in the numerous handicraft workshops which sprang up under the impetus of growing foreign trade and factory production. These small-scale factories, typically with a handful of workers and employing no mechanical power, processed agricultural products for export (e.g., cotton ginning, re-reeling of raw silk); sup-plied modern factories with simple parts and assemblies as subcontrac-tors; or ventured to produce coarser and cheaper versions of factory-made goods (e.g., textiles, cigarettes, matches, flour).[38] In other words, a significant part of China's early industrialization--like that of Japan--took the form not of a full-scale duplication of the foreign model, but of adaptations to China's factor endowment which were characterized by a high labor-capital ratio.

Some handicrafts did not survive the competition. Imported kero-sene very nearly replaced vegetable oils for lighting purposes. Silk weaving, which had prospered in the first quarter of the century, de-clined from the late 1920s as a consequence of Japanese competition, the loss of such markets as Manchuria after 1931, the advent of rayon, and the general depression of the international market.[39] The fall in tea exports in the 1920s and 1930s probably indicated that that industry was in trouble, although we know little about changes in domestic demand. In neither the case of silk nor that of tea, however, was there a simple linear decline from the nineteenth century attributable to the displacement of handicrafts by factory products.

In the case of cotton textile handicrafts one can be more specific. A recent study by Bruce Reynolds, which I believe supersedes all previous estimates, finds that the absolute output of handicraft yarn as well as the handicraft share in total yarn supply fell precipitously between 1875 and 1905, then more slowly to 1919, followed by another sharp drop to 1931 (table 8).[40] Handicraft weaving, in contrast, while its relative share dropped somewhat over the period 1875-1931, actually increased its total production in square yards during this half century. On the side of demand, this strong showing was due to the existence of partially discrete markets for the handicraft cloth--typically woven with imported and domestic machine-spun warp threads and, until the enormous growth of domestic spinning mills in the 1920s, handspun woofs-- and machine-loomed cloths of a finer quality. From the side of supply, the survival and growth of handicraft weaving is attributable to its integral role in the family farming production system of pre-1949 China. The key was the availability of "surplus" labor, specifically household labor which had a claim to subsistence in any case and, unlike factory labor, would be employed in handicraft activities even if its marginal product was below the cost of subsistence. Household handicrafts, that is, could meet the competition of factory industry at almost any price so long as the modern firm had to pay subsistence wages to its workers and craft workers had no income-earning alternatives. Rural families seeking to maximize income moved into and out of various activities supplementary to farming depending on their estimates of the relative advantages of each, which accounts in part for the variable fates of individual handicrafts. The technology of handicraft weaving, which advanced significantly in the twentieth century with the diffusion of improved wooden looms, iron-gear looms, and Jacquard looms, made possible a labor productivity much higher than in handicraft spinning. Inexpensive imported and domestic machine-spun yarn made handicraft spinning increasingly disadvantageous in relation to other sideline occupations. The combination of the availability and low cost of machine-spun yarn, the example of machine-loomed products, and the comparative advantage of weaving over spinning led to a shift into weaving by rural families. In such handicraft weaving centers as Ting-hsien, Pao-ti, and Kao-yang in Hopei, and Wei-hsien in Shantung, which experienced "booms" at various times in the 1920s and 1930s, large numbers of peasant households were supplied with yarn from Tientsin, Tsingtao,

TABLE 8

SOURCES OF COTTON CLOTH AND COTTON YARN SUPPLIES, 1875-1931

	1875		1905		1929		1931	
		Cotton	Cloth	Supply	(Million	Square	Yards)	
Manufactures	--	----%	27	1.1%	158	5.8%	831	28.2%
Imports	457	21.8	509	20.2	787	28.7	300	10.2
Handicrafts	1637	78.2	1981	78.7	1798	65.5	1815	61.6
Total	2094	100.0%	2517	100.0%	2743	100.0%	2946	100.0%
		Cotton	Yarn	Supply	(Million	Pounds)		
Manufactures	---	----%	90.2	11.5%	297.6	36.8%	966.9	90.9%
Imports	12.4	1.9	304.3	38.6	178.5	22.0	(-76.0)	(-7.1)
Handicrafts	632.3	98.1	393.2	49.9	333.6	41.2	173.3	16.3
Total	644.7	100.0%	787.7	100.0%	809.7	100.0%	1064.2	100.0%

Source: Bruce Lloyd Reynolds, "The Impact of Trade and Foreign Investment on Industrialization: Chinese Textiles, 1875-1931," Ph.D. dissertation, The University of Michigan, 1974, table 2.4, p. 31.

and Shanghai mills. Sometimes these households were also supplied with looms by textile merchants who contracted for their output and distributed it throughout north China and Manchuria. [41]

It is of considerable importance to our received picture of the fate of handicrafts in the twentieth century that many of the better quality field surveys of rural China date from the 1930s, that is, from the brief heyday of prewar academic scholarship. After almost two decades of political disruption, this period was seen as a hopeful time when China could at last embark on the journey to modern economic growth which had brought wealth and power to the West and Japan. To an impressively unanimous degree, China's economists and rural sociologists (even the majority who were not Marxists in outlook) tended to be as much concerned with the welfare implications of the functioning of the economic system as with analyzing its interrelationships and measuring its performance. That agricultural production roughly kept up with population growth, or that the absolute output of handicrafts at least held its own, in no way compensated for the observable facts that China's economy was "backward," most Chinese were poor while a very few were rich, and even the low standard of living of the poor was subject to severe uncertainties and fluctuations. Prosperity, moreover--the "demonstration effect" was powerful--could be achieved only through large-scale modern industrialization. In this context, there occurred both a disproportionate attention to the small modern sector and, even though the empirical data which were honestly presented frequently contradicted it, a tendency to draw conclusions from the declining phases of a cyclically fluctuating handicraft performance while ignoring the rising phases. [42] It was almost as if the more bankrupt the traditional sector could be shown to be, the more likely it was that a national effort to modernize and industrialize would be undertaken. The early 1930s were in all likelihood a relatively depressed period for the handicraft textile industry among others, but this lull does not appear to have been caused so much by the competition from modern mills as by the loss of the market in Manchuria and Jehol after 1931. To suggest that there was no recovery by 1936-1937 as a result of the development of alternative markets goes beyond what we presently know and contradicts the upward trend of the Chinese economy as a whole in the two years before the outbreak of war in mid-1937. And for the long and bitter years of war and civil war between 1937 and 1949, is it believable that modern and urban consumers' goods factories suffered less destruction and curtailment of output than the vast and decentralized handicraft sector?

Given the growth of imports and of the output of domestic factories, the fate of handicraft production in absolute terms depended on two factors: the structure of imports and of factory production, and the size and composition of aggregate demand. In 1925, for example, at most 50.5 percent of imports were competitive with handicrafts--cotton goods, cotton yarn, wheat flour, sugar, tobacco, paper, chemicals, dyes, and pigments (see table 28, p. 104). Apart from cotton goods and kerosene whose effects have already been noted, the largest remaining categories are sugar (whose importation was exceptionally high in 1925 and which includes unprocessed sugar not competitive with handicrafts); chemicals, dyes, and pigments (only a small part of which replaced indigenous dye-stuffs); and tobacco (the domestic processing of which increased in the 1920s and thus clearly was not swamped by imports). Other potentially competitive imports were minute and could not have seriously affected domestic handicrafts.

With respect to the impact of factory production, again excluding the case of cotton yarn in which handicraft output was sharply curtailed, the situation is similar. The most important handicraft products in 1933 were milled rice and wheat flour, which together accounted for 67 percent of the identified gross output value of all handicrafts. Of the total production of milled rice and wheat flour plus wheat flour imports, 95 percent came from the handicraft sector. If there had been any decline since the beginning of the century as a result of competition from modern food product factories or imports, it could not have been a very significant one. [43]

Knowing as little as we do about the domestic market for handi-crafts, it is difficult to speak directly about the pattern of aggregate demand in the republican era. Three indirect indicators, however, may be useful. China's population increased at an average annual rate of almost 1 percent between 1912 and 1949, while the growth rate of the urban population may have been as much as 2 percent. Population increase alone, and especially the growth of the coastal commercial and manufacturing centers, was adequate to account for a large part of the consumption of imported or domestic factory-made commodities. A significant portion of modern manufactures consisted of urban consumption goods which had little value in rural China. Even for items in universal use such as cotton textiles, product differentiation based on quality and cost was important. With respect to traditional demand, factory goods might be "inferior" goods. And if this was not the case, the rural population continued to use the products of handicraft industry when, given low wage rates and the high price of capital, these were produced at a lower unit cost than those produced by modern industry.

A second indicator is the persistence of external demand until the 1930s. One study reports that the value of handicraft exports in constant

1913 prices increased at a rate of about 2.6 percent a year between 1875 and 1928. Another estimate suggests an annual increase of 1.1 percent a year from 1912 to 1931 for a somewhat broader group of handicraft products.[44] Without more knowledge of domestic consumption, figures reporting increased exports are, of course, inconclusive. In the case of silk, however, which was China's largest single export in the 1920s, there are strong indications that in absolute terms the domestic market grew along with exports until 1930 while their relative shares were more or less constant.[45]

Finally, farm output, especially cash crops (many of which required processing), increased at about the same rate as population-- slightly below 1 percent a year--between 1912 and 1949. Perkins estimates the annual gross value of farm output in 1914-1918 at Ch$ 16.01– 17.03 billion, and in 1931-1937 at Ch$ 19.14—19.79 billion, a total increase of perhaps 16 to 19 percent over two decades.[46] He also argues that "no more than five or six per cent of farm output could have been processed in modern factories in the 1930's, or less than half the percentage of increase in farm output between the 1910's and 1930's."[47] At worst, in other words, handicraft processing of agricultural products held its own. In sum, anyone who would claim that the Hunan or Szechwan peasant in the 1930s dressed in Naigaiwata cottons, smoked BAT cigarettes, and used Meiji sugar has a big case to prove.

With respect to factory industry, in addition to its relatively small quantitative importance, several other general characteristics are worthy of attention:

1. Modern manufacturing industry, as I have already noted, tended to be concentrated in the coastal provinces, in particular in the treaty port cities, and after 1931 in Manchuria. In the all-important cotton textile industry, 87.0 percent of all spindles in China and 91.1 percent of all looms in 1924 were located in the provinces of Hopei, Liaoning, Shantung, Kiangsu, Chekiang, Fukien, and Kwangtung. The three cities of Shanghai, Tientsin, and Tsingtao accounted for 67.7 percent and 71.9 percent of spindles and looms respectively. While there was some geographical dispersion of, for example, cotton spindles in the 1930s (in 1918, 61.8 percent of the total spindles were located in Shanghai; in 1932, 55.4 percent; and in 1935, 51.1 percent), modern factory industry remained almost totally unknown in the interior provinces of China before the outbreak of the war with Japan.

2. One reason for the geographical concentration in the coastal provinces was the very large share which foreign-owned factories occupied

within the manufacturing sector. Foreign entrepreneurs had been permitted to establish factories in China since the Treaty of Shimonoseki in 1895, but these plants were restricted to the treaty ports. Between 1931 and 1945 the Manchurian economy was not linked to the rest of the Chinese economy, but it was precisely in Manchuria--if anywhere--that modern China experienced a degree of "economic development," including the construction of a substantial base of heavy industry. While the prominence of foreign-owned factories in China's prewar manufacturing industry is acknowledged by all sources, estimates of exactly how important they were in terms of their share of total output vary quite widely. Combining D. K. Lieu's survey data with other sources, Liu and Yeh have proposed the following figures for the gross value of output and number of workers in Chinese- and foreign-owned factories in China proper and Manchuria in 1933 (table 9).

TABLE 9

OUTPUT AND NUMBER OF WORKERS IN CHINESE-
AND FOREIGN-OWNED FACTORIES, 1933

	Gross Value of Output (Millions Chinese $)	Percentage	Number of Workers (1,000s)	Percentage
China Proper				
Chinese-owned	1,771.4	66.9	783.2	72.8
Foreign-owned	497.4	18.8	163.1	15.2
Manchuria	376.7	14.3	129.5	12.0
Total	2,645.5	100.0	1,075.8	100.0

Source: Table 4, p. 20.

For China proper alone, 78 percent of the output of factory industry was accounted for by Chinese-owned firms. This is a substantially higher proportion than the Chinese-owned share of the capitalization of manufacturing industry in China which, according to one rather crude estimate, was only 37 percent of the total in the 1930s.[48] The question arises as to whether the significance of foreign-owned industry in China is better measured by its share of output, or by the relative size of foreign capital investment as compared with Chinese investment. Excessive attention to capitalization, which in any case is notoriously difficult to measure, tends to exaggerate the importance of foreign-owned industry by slighting the fact that Chinese-owned industry was primarily light manufacturing in which the problem of capital indivisibility was minimal and the degree to which labor could be substituted for capital was quite large--in other words, by implicitly assuming the same capital-output ratio in Chinese- and foreign-owned factories. Table 10 gives some indication of the output share of foreign enterprises in several branches of manufacturing industry in the 1920s and 1930s. (See also table 3, page 14, for 1933.) Data on coal mining are included here; in general, apart from the matter of concentration in the treaty ports, what is being said about factories applies as well to mining.

3. Factory industry in China exclusive of Manchuria was predominantly consumers' goods industry. In 1933 producers' goods accounted for 25 percent of net value added by factories. The largest industries, as measured by the value of their output, were cotton textiles, flour milling, cigarettes, and oil pressing. Among the 2,435 Chinese-owned factories investigated by D. K. Lieu, 50 percent were engaged in the manufacture of textiles and foodstuffs. These 1,211 plants as a group accounted for 76 percent of the value of output, 71 percent of the employment, 60 percent of the power installed, and 58 percent of the capital investment of all Chinese-owned factories.

4. The average size of factories was small, and generally smaller for Chinese- than foreign-owned firms in the same industry, but not very small as compared, for example, with Japanese plants in the Meiji era or with the early industrial experience of other countries. The 2,435 factories surveyed by D. K. Lieu had a total capitalization of Ch$406 million, giving an average of Ch$166,000 or about US$50,000 at the prevailing exchange rate. These plants had a total motive power capacity of 507,300 hp or about 200 hp per factory. The average number of workers per factory was 202.

5. Of the Chinese-owned factories, even those located in the treaty ports, it may be said that the social context in which they existed and which impinged importantly on the "modern" fact that they employed mechanical power and complex machinery remained to a remarkable extent "traditional." Only 612 of D. K. Lieu's 2,435 factories were organized as joint-stock companies. The absence of a well-developed market for the transfer of equity shares contributed to a particular relationship between shareholders and management in which the demands of

TABLE 10

PERCENTAGE OF TOTAL OUTPUT BY CHINESE AND FOREIGN FIRMS IN SELECTED INDUSTRIES

Year	Coal[a]		Cotton Yarn		Cotton Cloth		Cigarettes		Electric Power		Matches	
	Chinese	Foreign	Chinese	Foreign	Chinese	Foreign	Chinese	Foreign	Chinese	Foreign	Chinese	Foreign
1913	7.0	93.0	--	--	--	--	--	--	--	--	--	--
1919	24.4	75.6	57	43	41	59	--	--	--	--	--	--
1923	21.1	78.9	67	33	50	50	--	--	23	77	--	--
1928	22.0	78.0	62	38	44	56	--	--	--	--	--	--
1933	16.7	83.3	71	29	39	61	43	57	37	63	89	11
1936	34.3	65.7	71	29	36	64	42[b]	58[b]	45	55	89[b]	11[b]

Sources: Yen Chung-ping, Chung-kuo chin-tai ching-chi shih t'ung-chi tzu-liao hsuan-chi, pp. 124, 130-131; Reynolds, "The Impact of Trade and Foreign Investment on Industrialization: Chinese Textiles, 1875-1931," pp. 216, 221; Ch'en Chen, Chung-kuo chin-tai kung-yeh shih tzu-liao [Source materials on China's modern industrial history], 4 vols. (Peking: San-lien, 1957-1961), vol. 2, p. 971.

Note: Foreign refers to foreign-owned or foreign-investment/control industries.

[a] "Modern" mines only.

[b] 1935.

the former for short-term profits often adversely affected long-term expansion and modernization through reinvestment. Such practices as guaranteed dividends frequently forced firms to borrow at high rates in order to obtain working capital. Financing for modern industry was never adequate in republican China. Investment in agricultural land and urban real estate continued to be attractive; to these were added in more recent times speculation in commodities, foreign exchange, and government bonds. We shall see below how government fiscal policy tended to divert funds from productive investment.

Competent management was in short supply. Only five hundred of some four thousand technicians in eighty-two spinning mills in 1931 had received formal training. Higher management was not greatly different from what it had been in the kuan-tu shang-pan period. Such techniques as cost accounting were sparsely employed: two-story factory buildings on cheap land were not uncommon, and the inadequacy of allowances for depreciation and the repair of equipment is noted by almost all observers. Such circumstances, however, have been characteristic of the early stages of industrialization throughout the world and were not particularly worse in China than, say, in the American textile industry fifty years earlier.

Foremen in Chinese factories tended to retain a "long-gown" attitude, disdained to engage in menial tasks, and left the actual supervision of workers to technically incompetent overseers who frequently were also "contractors" who had recruited the workers by, for example, making arrangements with the parents of child laborers. While there were over a million factory workers by 1933, this was overall not a skilled, stable, or disciplined labor force. Sectoral variations were probably significant, as in Japan. Where experience counted, it was rewarded. Highly skilled male workers were well-paid, well-trained, and tended to stay with one employer. In the dominant textile industry, however, experience was not critically important, except for mechanics. Many workers retained their ties with the agricultural villages which, under force of necessity, they had left in order to supplement a meager farming income with factory wages. This was especially true of the young women and children who formed a very high proportion of the labor force. The 493,257 workers in D. K. Lieu's 2,435 factories included 202,762 men, 243,435 women, and 47,060 children under sixteen; for the textile industry, the comparable figures were 84,767, 187,947, and 29,758. With a labor force not fully committed to a lifetime in a factory, and with a potentially plentiful supply of workers available from the peasantry, industrial wages were low by international stan-

dards and hours were long. Chinese textile mills before 1937 typically operated on two twelve-hour shifts; eleven-hour shifts were
general in Japanese-owned mills. The real income of the urban
worker, however, was high by rural Chinese standards, which was
why migration to the cities was sustained. In circumstances where
capital was expensive and labor cheap, "rationalization" of production in some Chinese firms took the form of more intensive use of
labor by lowering wages and lengthening hours. The prevalence of
low wage rates perpetuated a high labor turnover and made the worker reluctant to sever all ties with his village which continued to offer
him a refuge in times of industrial slowdown. This then neatly confirmed the employer's belief that the worker could live on a "handful
of rice." The convention of low wages, moreover, partly justified
itself by preventing a rise in labor efficiency.[49]

It probably could not have been otherwise. One fundamental
problem faced by Chinese industry was the weakness of demand. As
long as, outside of the treaty ports and their immediate environs,
the traditional society and impoverished peasant economy continued
basically unchanged, what market could there be for new or improved
(and costlier) goods produced with well-paid labor?

6. The concentration of Chinese industry in coastal cities, the large
foreign-owned component, the predominance of consumers' goods,
and the small size and technical backwardness of most factories are
all correlates of the very small share of modern industry in China's
national product before 1949. But to estimate that the modern share
of M^+ (factory output, mining, utilities, modern transportation) accounted for only 5 percent (table 2) or 7 percent (table 3) of total
domestic product in the 1930s--i.e., that China's economy was clearly an "underdeveloped" one--should not lead to the conclusion that
this modern industrial and transport sector was of no consequence
for China's post-1949 economic development. If what the People's
Republic of China inherited was quantitatively small, nevertheless
over two-thirds of the increase in industrial production during 1953-
1957 came from the expanded output of existing factories.[50] In spite
of Soviet removals of industrial machinery and equipment from Manchuria, the new investment necessary to restore output in this major
producers' goods base was less than would have been required for
entirely new plants. If, as a whole, pre-1949 China was not indus-
trialized, its cotton textile industry grew rapidly and steadily and
was not monopolized by foreign-owned firms. Even in the 1930s,
China's cotton textile output was one of the largest in the world.
After 1949, although new investment in consumers' goods industry

lagged far behind producers' goods, the exportation of textile fabrics and clothing was--next to raw and processed agricultural products--a major source of the foreign exchange which paid for China's importation of consumers' goods. [51]

Equally important, the small pre-1949 modern sector provided the PRC with skilled workers and technicians, experienced managers, and patterns of organized activity which, supplemented by Soviet advisors and training, made it possible to provide training and experience to the vastly expanded number of new managers and workers who were to staff the many new factories that began production in the late 1950s. In the producers' goods sector, in particular, the dozens of relatively small Shanghai machine-building firms--many inherited from the pre-1949 period--retained a qualitative flexibility to develop new products and techniques. This flexibility allowed them to play a large role in overcoming the difficulties in the early 1960s that stemmed from the Great Leap Forward and the withdrawal of Soviet advisors and blueprints. [52] "Without this base, China's industrial development in the 1950's and 1960's would have been significantly slower or would have had to rely more heavily on foreign technicians, or both." [53]

VI. Agriculture

China's economy in the republican era, as it had been in the past, was overwhelmingly agricultural. Net value added by agriculture in 1933 amounted to Ch$ 18.76 billion or 65 percent of the total net domestic product. This output was produced by 205 million agricultural workers, 79 percent of the labor force. Between 1912 and 1933, only small changes occurred in the share of domestic product attributable to agriculture and in the proportion of the labor force engaged in farming, although after 1933 the share of agriculture declined somewhat more rapidly than in earlier years, in large part as a result of rapid industrial growth in Manchuria (see table 3, page 14). Plant products dominated, and within this category food crops were overwhelmingly important. For 1933, for example, the estimates shown in table 11 have been offered. By weight, a rough measure to be sure, food crops (rice, wheat, other grains, potatoes, vegetables, and fruits) accounted for 80 percent of the output of plant products.

Until 1937 the total output of agriculture, with sometimes important annual and regional fluctuations due to natural and man-made calamities, approximately kept pace with the growth of population from 430

TABLE 11

OUTPUT OF THE SEVERAL SECTORS OF AGRICULTURE, 1933

	Gross Value Added (Billions Chinese $)
Plant products	15.73
Animal products	1.37
Forest products	0.60
Fishery products	0.41
Miscellaneous products	1.07
Total	19.18
(Less depreciation)	(0.42)
Net value added	18.76

Source: Liu and Yeh, The Economy of the Chinese Mainland, table 36, p. 140.

million in 1912 to 500 million in the mid-1930s. The per capita value in constant prices of farm output in 1931-1937 was about the same as it had been in 1914-1918 (table 12), reflecting an output increase of a little less than 1 percent a year. In part this increment resulted from an expansion of cultivated land area which Perkins estimates at 1,356 million shih mou in 1918 and 1,471 million shih mou in 1933.[54] The balance came from increases in the output of grains and from augmented production of cash crops on existing land. Grain output per capita remained unchanged at about Ch$ 21 during this whole period while the per capita output of other products, including cash crops, increased from Ch$ 15 to Ch$ 17. Table 13 shows the changes in physical output quantities of plant products during 1914-1957. From 1914-1918 to 1931-1937 all grains (in catties; each catty equals 1.1 pounds) increased by 12.9 percent; but rice output fell 5.8 percent, while the production of potatoes and corn grew by 16.4 percent and 39.2 percent, respectively. These changes reflect a shift of cropping patterns to the production of plant products which yielded more calories per unit of land, thus releasing land for the increased cultivation of cash crops. Wheat, the

TABLE 12

GROSS VALUE OF FARM OUTPUT, 1914-1957
(Billions 1933 Chinese $)

	1914-1918 (average year)	1931-1937 (average year)	1957
Grain	9.15-10.17	10.31-10.96	12.32
Soybeans	0.43	0.66	0.78
Oil-bearing crops	0.51	1.13	0.77
Cotton and other fibers	0.78	0.86	1.28
Tobacco, tea, and silk	0.49	0.52	0.32
Sugarcane and beets	0.11	0.11	0.14
Animals	1.14	1.40	2.74
Subtotal	13.63	15.65	19.36
Other products	3.40	4.14	4.91
Total Gross Value	16.01-17.03	19.14-19.79	24.27
Per capita (Ch$)	36.1-38.4	38.1-39.4	37.5

Source: Perkins, Agricultural Development in China, table II.8, p. 30.

output of which grew by 16.8 percent, was a cash crop in some areas of north China where it was marketed to provide cash for rougher grains such as kaoliang and millet for farm consumption. In north and central China wheat and cotton impinged on rice acreage, while in central China oil seed-bearing crops were also augmented. Cash crop output accounted for approximately 14 percent of farm output by value in 1914-1918 and 17 percent in 1931-1937, while the physical output of individual industrial crops increased more rapidly than grains: sesame, 170.1 percent; soybeans, 53.7 percent; rapeseed, 33.7 percent; cotton, 17.6 percent; peanuts, 15.6 percent; and tobacco, 15.1 percent.[55]

In addition to supporting a slowly growing rural population, China's prewar agriculture in "normal" times supplied part of the food and raw materials needs of the urban areas which were growing somewhat more rapidly. Transportation and other disruptions resulting from civil war in the 1920s required increasing supplementation of urban consumption with imported grains. Imports then dropped off somewhat in the 1930s before rising again with the advent of war.[56] Agricultural commodities,

TABLE 13

PHYSICAL OUTPUT OF PLANT PRODUCTS, 1914-1957
(1, 000, 000 catties)

	1914-1919 (average year)	1931-1937 (average year)	1957
Rice	147, 610	139, 110	173, 600
Wheat	39, 570	46, 200	47, 100
Corn	14, 680	20, 440	37, 470
Potatoes [a]	7, 060	15, 280	43, 800
Kaoliang	23, 750	24, 680	20, 030
Millet	22, 180	27, 680	23, 330
Barley	18, 090	19, 440	9, 300
Other grain	10, 370	10, 940	15, 170
Total grain	283, 300	319, 960	370, 000
Soybeans	10, 970	16, 860	20, 100
Peanuts	4, 540	5, 250	5, 142
Rapeseed	3, 800	5, 080	1, 775
Sesame	670	1, 810	625
Cotton	1, 606	1, 888	3, 280
Fibers	1, 410	1, 350	1, 290
Tobacco	1, 590	1, 830	1, 220
Sugarcane	18, 720	18, 720	20, 785
Sugarbeets	---	---	3, 002
Tea	445	399	223
Silk	406	420	225

Source: Perkins, Agricultural Development in China, pp. 266-289.

[a] Grain equivalents.

moreover, accounted for the bulk of China's exports (see table 28, page 104). As a whole exports grew 3.5 percent a year in value and 1.7 percent a year in quantity during the period 1912-1931.[57] All told, this was a creditable performance for an agricultural sector which experienced no significant technological improvements before 1949. For individual farm families or particular localities and regions, of course, the annual outcome was not so uniform during the four decades of the republican era. Output and income could fluctuate greatly due to weather, natural disasters, destructive war and civil war, or unfavorable price trends.[58] Barely adequate overall production left no margin of protection against such all-too-frequent contingencies, nor against the frightening uncertainty from year to year of whether one's family would be fed. Even the "creditable performance" requires some explanation, and then further qualification.

Amano Motonosuke's magistral history of Chinese agriculture, which carefully examines the technology associated with each major crop as well as the development of farming implements, impressively demonstrates that the agricultural technology of the republican era was a continuation, with few improvements, of the farming practices of the Ch'ing period.[59] Scattered efforts to develop improved seeds and demonstrate better farm practices can be noted throughout the republican years. For example, 251 agricultural experiment stations were established in the provinces during 1912-1927.[60] The Nanking government's Bureau of Commerce and Industry, and later the Bureau of Agriculture and Mining and the National Economic Council, also encouraged agricultural research and the diffusion of agronomic knowledge.[61] These efforts, however, were small in scale and their effectiveness severely constrained by the lack of support from local government.

The slow growth of total farm production in the first decades of the twentieth century shown in tables 12 and 13 was not to any important degree the result of better seeds, increased and improved fertilizers, or significant additions to irrigation and water control. Seventy percent of the increase in cultivated acreage between 1913 and the 1930s occurred in Manchuria, in particular through the expansion of acreage for soybeans, kaoliang, and other grains consumed by a population which grew from about eighteen million in 1910 to thirty-eight million in 1940.[62] That is, the extensive development of Manchurian agriculture employing "traditional" technology accounted for a large share of the increase in total farm output. Small acreage increases also were experienced in Kiangsu, Hupei, Yunnan, and Szechwan, but for the most part other increments to output were the result of the adoption of the best traditional farming practices in areas which had hitherto operated at a less than optimum production possibility surface consistent with their resources. Part (and perhaps most) of the increased yields on existing cropland came from the application of more labor. The more intensive cultivation of some food grains, and especially the augmented production of cash crops, reflect this remaining but limited growth possibility within the traditional technology.

Both the opening of the Manchurian frontier and the more intensive exploitation of traditional practices were facilitated by the responsiveness of the Chinese farm family to rising export demand, favorable price trends, and the availability of urban off-farm employment opportunities, all of which persisted until the depression of the early 1930s. That the increased agricultural output which resulted was adequate statistically to feed China's population was so because the rate of population growth was a very modest one--on the average less than 1 percent a year. This slow growth itself resulted from a relatively high birthrate in combination with a high but fluctuating death rate which reflected a generally low standard of living, poor public health conditions, and high susceptibility to the effects of natural and man-made disasters. One approaches the paradox that agricultural output was adequate in the sense defined only because the average Chinese remained poor and population growth was subject to Malthusian controls. Within these direful limits, the demand for cash crops for export and by industries in the urban sector (which could be responded to because of the developments in transportation which I discuss below) permitted some degree of shifting to the production of crops yielding a higher income per unit of land, especially by smaller size farms.

Prices were favorable to the farmer until 1931; table 14 presents the essential data. The general trend was upward during the first three decades of the century--prices of agricultural products, goods purchased by the farmer for both production and consumption, land values, farm wages, and taxes all increased. While the terms of trade between agriculture and manufactured goods fluctuated in the 1910s, they were increasingly favorable to agriculture in the 1920s, indicating that prices received by the farmer rose even more rapidly than the prices he paid. Agricultural prices increased by 116 percent (if one uses Buck's index in table 14) between 1913 and 1931, while prices paid by farmers rose by 108 percent. In the same period land values increased by 63 percent, farm wages by 75 percent, and land taxes by 67 percent. Wages tended to lag behind prices in north China but more nearly kept up with prices in the southern rice region, indicating a greater demand for labor and relatively more nonfarm employment opportunities in south China. Where prices stayed ahead of wages, the farmer employing hired labor clearly profited more from the higher prices he received for his crops. Land values and land taxes increased least of all in these two decades. It appears to be the case that the real as opposed to the monetary burden of land taxes declined during these decades of generally rising prices.

From 1931 until recovery began in 1935 and continued in 1936, however, Chinese farmers experienced a sharp fall in income and a

TABLE 14

INDEX NUMBERS OF AGRICULTURAL PRICES, TERMS OF TRADE, LAND VALUES, FARM WAGES, AND LAND TAX, 1913–1937

(1926 = 100)

| Year | (1) Agricultural Products, Wholesale Prices | | | (2) Terms of Trade | | | | | (3) Land Values | | (4) Farm Wages | (5) Land Tax |
| | Tientsin | Shanghai | China [a] | (1) ÷ Wholesale Prices of All Manufactured Goods | | (1) ÷ Wholesale Prices of Consumers' Goods | | (1) ÷ Prices Paid by Farmers | Buck | NARB | | |
				Tientsin	Shanghai	Tientsin	Shanghai	China [a]				
1913	61	--	58	82	--	86	--	89	63	--	72	79
1914	58	--	59	78	--	83	--	92	66	--	74	80
1915	58	--	61	74	--	81	--	90	68	--	77	84
1916	61	--	65	72	--	81	--	92	72	--	80	86
1917	70	--	69	77	--	88	--	91	75	--	83	83
1918	64	--	69	67	--	74	--	87	77	--	86	84
1919	59	--	69	61	--	63	--	84	81	--	88	86
1920	77	--	80	76	--	79	--	94	83	--	89	87
1921	78	75	90	77	66	80	76	102	87	--	91	86
1922	75	86	92	78	83	78	90	101	89	--	93	86
1923	82	92	98	84	86	83	91	103	92	--	95	88
1924	89	92	97	90	92	90	94	96	95	--	95	89
1925	100	95	102	101	94	102	95	101	100	--	97	92
1926	100	100	100	100	100	100	100	100	100	--	100	100
1927	103	103	95	101	98	98	98	92	100	--	105	109
1928	103	95	106	97	92	94	92	97	96	--	112	118

1929	107	99	127	96	94	94	96	108	100	--	118	119
1930	107	113	125	90	98	81	101	99	99	--	124	140
1931	96	106	116	72	80	70	82	86	103	100[b]	126	132
1932	90	95	103	73	79	69	80	81	93	95	--	--
1933	73	94	--	64	84	61	86	--	--	89	--	--
1934	64	86	--	60	83	59	84	--	--	82	--	--
1935	82	83	--	79	83	75	82	--	--	81	--	--
1936	102	102	--	87	91	82	91	--	--	84	--	--
1937	--	140	--	--	106	--	108	--	--	--	--	--

Sources: (1) and (2), Nankai Institute of Economics, Nan-k'ai chih-su tzu-liao hui pien [Nankai index numbers] (Peking: T'ung-chi, 1958), pp. 12–13; Shanghai chieh-fang ch'ien hou wu-chia tzu-liao hui-pien [Shanghai prices before and after Liberation] (Shanghai: Jen-min, 1958), p. 135; J. L. Buck, Land Utilization in China, Statistics (Nanking: University of Nanking, 1937), pp. 149–150. (3) Buck, Statistics, pp. 168–169; Nung-ch'ing pao-kao, 7.4 (April 1939), p. 47, in Chang Yu-i, comp., Chung-kuo chin-tai nung-yeh shih tzu-liao [Source materials on China's modern agricultural history] (Peking: San-lien, 1957), vol. 3, pp. 708–710. (4) Buck, Statistics, p. 151. (5) Buck, Statistics, p. 167.

[a] Thirty-seven localities in 36 hsien in 15 provinces.

[b] 1931=100.

striking reversal of the terms of trade. These consequences were
brought on by both the contraction of export markets resulting from the
world depression (the effects were delayed in China as silver prices
continued to fall until 1931) and the outflow of silver from China as the
gold price of silver rose from 1931, pushed upward first by the depar-
ture of England, Japan, and the United States from the gold standard
and then by the U.S. Silver Purchase Act of 1934. In this period of
steeply falling prices, the farmer's fixed costs and the prices of manufactured goods tended to be more "sticky" than prices received for
agricultural commodities which fell first and more rapidly. There was
a clear tendency for farmers to cut back on cash crop production and
return to the cultivation of traditional grain crops in response to the
depression.[63] Opportunities for off-farm employment, which had been
essential to the family incomes of small farmers in particular, also
may have declined temporarily after 1931 with a resulting flow of labor
back to rural areas from the cities.[64] Data on farm wages are sporadic,
but wages probably fell less than agricultural prices. Land taxes on the
average increased by 8 to 10 percent during 1931-1934 (and then declined in 1935 and 1936), while land values fell from 1931, which meant
an increase in the farmer's real tax burden during the depression.[65]
The outflow of silver from rural areas to Shanghai and other cities
made it more burdensome for farmers to obtain loans. In sum, significant parts of the gains that had accrued to the agricultural sector
during the previous long inflationary phase were lost in 1931-1935.
Recovery of both agricultural prices and cash crop output was under-
way by 1936, but very little time intervened before the Japanese invasion and full-scale war in mid-1937 introduced a somewhat different
set of agricultural problems.

How many farm families were affected, and to what degree, favor-
ably by the general rise of prices to 1931 and negatively by the precipi-
tous decline--by almost 25 percent--during 1931-1935 depends of course
on the degree to which agriculture was commercialized or involved in
market transactions. Perkins has estimated that in the 1920s and 1930s
20 to 30 percent of farm output was sold locally, another 10 percent
shipped to urban areas, and 3 percent exported--an increase in the latter
two categories from 5 to 7 percent and 1 to 2 percent respectively before 1910. Increasing commercialization in the twentieth century is
attested to also by qualitative data compiled by Chang Yu-i, although
his primary purpose is to illustrate the deleterious consequences for
China's peasants of the activities of both indigenous and foreign imperialist merchants.[66] Yet, outside of the more commercialized regions--
say the Yangtze provinces--and apart from commercially minded rich

peasants, most farmers were still only marginally involved with markets. If we recall that cash crops (most of which were marketed) accounted for 17 percent of farm output in the 1930s, Perkins' estimate of the extent of commercialization implies that less than a quarter of food crop output was sold by farmers, and most of that in local markets little affected by international price trends. Even in Changsha, the major rice market in Hunan and one of China's largest, prices in the 1930s varied mainly with the state of the provincial harvest and local political conditions. In the majority of farming communities, even a national average decline of prices by 25 percent would have meant a much smaller drop in real income, maybe only by 5 percent. That is, the effect of the depression--and of other price fluctuations--in the interior provinces of China may have been no more calamitous than the inevitable fluctuations in the weather.

China's agriculture managed to keep the Chinese people alive, and even to produce a small "surplus" above minimum consumption levels. Overall, food consumption represented 60 percent of domestic expenditure by end use, while total personal consumption accounted for over 90 percent, leaving almost insignificant amounts for communal services, government consumption, and investment.[67] As the average per capita farm output of Ch$ 38-39 shown in table 12 indicates, this plainly remained a "poor" economy with minimal living standards for the mass of the population. China's grain yields per mou in the 1920s and 1930s were by no means low by international standards. Rice yields, for example, were slightly higher than those of early Meiji Japan--although 30 percent lower than Japan in the 1930s--and double or triple those of India and Thailand, while wheat yields were about the same as the United States. The average output of grain-equivalent per man-equivalent (one farmer working a full year) in China in the 1920s, however, was only 1,400 kilograms; the comparable figure for the United States was 20,000 kilograms--fourteen times as large.[68] Here was the essential reason for China's poverty: four-fifths of the labor force was employed in agriculture, and the technical and organizational characteristics of this industry were such that the value added per worker was strikingly low both in comparison with developed economies and with the modern sector of China's economy.

The principal obstacle to accelerated industrialization in China's condition of economic "backwardness" was probably the failure of either the private sector or the Peking and Nanking governments to marshal and allocate the funds, resources, and technology required for significant and continued new investment. Annual gross investment in China proper probably never exceeded 5 percent of national product before 1949. Apart from the disabilities of the political leadership, China's continuing disunity, and the exigencies of war and civil war, the inability of the agricultural sector to increase output sufficiently to meet any greatly enhanced demands for urban food and raw material consumption and for exports to exchange for major new imports of industrial plants and machinery--while continuing to feed a growing rural population-- contributed to the slow rate of structural change. The alternative route of imposing drastic "forced savings" on a slowly growing agricultural sector was not in practice open to the weak governments of republican China.

Neither the "distributionist" nor the "technological" analysis of China's failure to industrialize before 1949, and in particular of the absence of significant growth in agriculture, is by itself satisfactory. The technological or "eclectic" approach rejects the notion that rural socio-economic relationships were responsible for the more intractable problems of the agricultural sector, and concludes--as I have done above--that on the whole the performance of agriculture before 1937 was a creditable one. To the extent that growth was inhibited, this is attributed to the unavailability of appropriate inputs--especially technological improvements--and not to institutional rigidities. [69] The emphasis of the distributionist approach is upon the contributions of unequal land ownership, tenancy, rural indebtedness, inequitable taxation, and allegedly monopolistic and monopsonistic markets to supposed agricultural stagnation and increasing impoverishment. It concludes that "lack of security of tenure, high rents and a one-sided relationship between landlord and tenant gave rise to a situation in which both the incentive and the material means to undertake net farm investment were lacking."[70] At a more general level, the distributionist school attributes China's "continuing rural stagnation" to "the siphoning off of income from the tiller of the soil and its unproductive expenditure by a variety of parasitic elements who lived on, but contributed nothing to, the rural surplus."[71]

There are at least two potential difficulties with a purely technological analysis. It may ignore the extremely low absolute levels of per capita output and income resulting from the modest expansion of agriculture which it recounts and thus ignore the urgency of demands for improvement. More importantly, it may be ahistorical in seeming to believe that adjustments, say of the agricultural production function by introducing improved technology, were potentially forthcoming within the given equilibrium system. But it was problematic indeed in repub-

lican China, even in the absence of war and civil war, that within any
reasonable time span significant new inputs would be available without
substantial institutional change toward a new equilibrium system.

Likewise, a number of shortcomings weaken a purely distributionist analysis. First, the progressive immiseration which is implied
is not supported by any studies of the overall performance of the agricultural sector during several decades. That individual farmers, localities, and even larger regions suffered severe difficulties of varying
duration is beyond doubt. This is not, however, evidence that, so long
as population growth remained low, the existing agricultural system
could not sustain itself at low and constant per capita output and income
levels. For how long may be a valid query--as is the ethical question
of the desirability that it should do so--but secular breakdown before
the destructive years between 1937 and 1949 is not proven.

There is a problem, too, about the proportion of the "surplus"
produced by agriculture potentially available for productive investment.
Following Lippit, who identifies the rural surplus with the property
income (mainly rents) received by landowners plus taxes paid by owner-
cultivators, Riskin finds the actual total rural surplus in 1933 equal to
19 percent of net domestic product. (The surplus produced by the nonagricultural sectors he estimates at 8.2 percent of NDP, giving a total
actual surplus of 27.2 percent of NDP.) There is a further assumption,
however, that after deducting the proportion of investment, communal
services, and government consumption attributable to the rural surplus
(1 percent out of a total of 5.8 percent of NDP for these purposes in
1933), 15 percent of NDP was utilized for luxury consumption by the
rural elite.[72] Indeed some part was so used, but other parts were
hoarded, "invested" in real estate, or reloaned to peasant borrowers.
The principal difficulty with assuming a rural surplus above mass consumption equivalent to 15 percent of NDP available for redistribution
is that neither Lippit nor Riskin nor I have any useful quantitative data
with which to estimate the importance of these various alternative uses
of the surplus. If, for example, net landlord purchases of agricultural
land and urban real estate, hoarding of gold and silver, and consumption
loans to farmers were large, this in effect involved a "recirculation" of
part of the landlords' income to peasant consumption. None of these
was a direct burden on consumption in a particular time period, although
in the longer run they may possibly have increased individual landlord
claims to a share of national income. Only the conspicuous consumption of the wealthy, in particular their spending on imported luxuries--
thereby depleting the foreign exchange resources which might otherwise

have been available for the purchase of capital goods--was an "exhaustive" expenditure, a direct drain on the domestic product.

And then, of course, the experience of China's agriculture in the first decade of the People's Republic should be evidence enough that while substantial social change may have been a necessary condition for sustained increases in output, it was far from being a sufficient one. Even with the post-1958 increased emphasis on investment in agriculture, China's farm output still lags. The problems of supplying better seed stock, adequate fertilizer and water, optimum cropping patterns, and mechanization at critical points of labor shortage have not been easily met. In sum, the whole experience of the first three-quarters of the twentieth century suggests that only with institutional reorganization and large doses of advanced technological input could China's agrarian problem be solved.

If the agrarian organization of the republican period cushioned rural China from the forced savings of an authoritarian regime, it did so by abandoning any hope that the lot of a farmer would ever be better than that which his father, and his father before him, had experienced. In other words, if the redistributive effects of peasant-landlord-government relations in rural China before 1949 were perhaps not so onerous for the peasantry as is generally believed, their long-term output effects were debilitating for the economy as a whole. Land tenure, rural usury, and regressive taxation were the natural issues around which sentiment could be mobilized for the overthrow of a social system which offered little prospect for betterment.

The estimates we have used for population (430 million in 1912, 500 million in the mid-1930s) and for cultivated acreage (1,356 million mou and 1,471 million mou) suggest that the area of cultivated land per capita decreased from 3.15 mou to 2.94 mou in the first decades of the twentieth century. Responses collected by Buck's investigators also indicate a decline from 1870 to 1933 in the size of the average farm operated. [73] Although derived from different sources and by different methods, the two estimates (1 mou = 0.1647 acre) are very close-- Buck: 2.62 acres (crop area) per farm family in 1910, 2.27 acres in 1933; Perkins (assuming an average household of five persons): 2.6 acres in 1913; 2.4 acres in the 1930s. The size distribution of farms operated as of 1934-1935 is shown in table 16(3). In the southern provinces (Buck's "Rice Region"), the average unit of cultivation tended to be substantially smaller than in the north (the "Wheat Region"). In all regions there was a significant correlation between size of household and farm size, an indication that high population density had forced the price of land so high that peasants could afford to till it only in a lavishly labor-using fashion. Therefore farm size was small when household members were few.

The uneconomic aspects of miniature cultivation were aggravated by the fact that farms tended to be broken up into several nonadjacent parcels, a product in large part of the absence of primogeniture in Chinese inheritance practices. Considerable land was wasted in boundary strips, excessive labor time was used in travel from parcel to parcel, and rational irrigation practices were made more difficult. Buck's average was six parcels per farm; other writers mention five to forty parcels.

While the Chinese farmer had skillfully exploited the traditional agricultural technology to the very limit of its possibilities, few of the nineteenth- and twentieth-century advances in seeds, implements, fertilizers, insecticides and the like had found their way into rural China. Investment in agriculture was overwhelmingly investment in land. Human power was more important than animal power, and the farmer's implements--little changed over the centuries--were adapted to human power. The utilization of human labor per acre of land was probably more intensive than in any other country of the world, while paradoxically the individual laborer was not intensively used except at peak periods such as planting or harvesting. Only 35 percent of rural men aged sixteen to sixty were engaged in full-time agricultural work, while 50 percent worked only part-time. Part of the surplus labor power was devoted to subsidiary occupations, usually home industry, which provided 14 percent of the income of farm families so engaged. [74]

The kind and quantity of agricultural output summarized at the beginning of this section were the results of the decisions as to the allocation of their human and material resources and the application of their farming skills by millions of peasant households. Nearly half of these family farms were less than ten mou (1.6 acres) in size, and 80 percent were smaller than thirty mou (5 acres). One must distinguish, however, between unit of cultivation and unit of ownership, and inquire what the effects of substantial tenancy and its conditions were on agricultural output and individual farm family welfare.

What was the extent of rented land in the 1930s? Buck, for example, estimated that 28.7 percent of privately owned farmland was rented to tenants (table 16(2)). If one adds to this the 6.7 percent of farmland that was publicly owned (kung-t'ien, government land, school land, temple land, ancestral land, soldiers' land, and charity land), which was almost entirely rented out, it appears that 35.5 percent of agricultural land was rented to tenants.[75] This estimate is confirmed by data on the quantity of land which was redistributed in the course of land reform in the first years of the People's Republic--from 42 to 44 percent of the cultivated area in 1952.[76] The proportion beyond 35.5 percent is perhaps an indication of the zeal with which land owned by "rich peasants" as well as landlords was confiscated during the land reform.

Land ownership in China was very unequal, but probably less so than in many other underdeveloped countries. The best data for the 1930s were obtained by a land survey in sixteen provinces (excluding Manchuria) conducted by the National Land Commission of the National Economic Council and the Ministries of Finance and Interior; these data are shown in table 15. Some downward bias is present in these figures as a consequence of including information only about landlords actually resident in the areas surveyed. The average holding of the 1,295,001 owners covered by this 1934-1935 survey was 15.17 mou (2.5 acres). But the 73 percent of the families surveyed who owned 15 mou or less held only 28 percent of the total land, while the 5 percent of the families who owned 50 mou or more held 34 percent of the total land.

Few of the large holdings were farmed as such by their owners; commercial farming with hired labor was a rarity. In general the land was leased to tenants, or part was farmed by the landlord (with the labor of his family and/or with hired labor, depending on the size of his holding and his social status) and the balance leased. The twentieth century, with the breakdown of civil order in many parts of the interior, saw an increase in the incidence of absentee landlords who abandoned the rural town for the protection of city walls. These landlords retained only a financial interest in their property and entrusted the supervision of tenants and rent collection to local agents (tsu-chan or "landlord bursaries" in the Yangtze Valley, for example) who often stood to profit the more they were able to "squeeze" their charges.[77] Hereby, particularly in the southern and eastern coastal provinces, was introduced an increasing element of harshness into rural class relations--never the subject for a pastoral idyll even under the best Confucian landlord, but possibly a little more personal and humane than under the inexorable pressure of the market.

Perkins suggests that in the 1930s three-quarters of rented-out land was owned outside of the village, by absentee landlords most of

TABLE 15

DISTRIBUTION OF RURAL LAND OWNERSHIP IN SIXTEEN PROVINCES, 1934-1935

Size Classes of Land Owned (mou)	Number of Families (hu) Surveyed	Percentage of Families Surveyed	Land Owned (1,000 mou)	Percentage of Land Owned	Average Land per Family (mou)
<5	461,128	35.61	1,217	6.21	2.64
5- 9.9	310,616	23.99	2,245	11.42	7.23
10- 14.9	170,604	13.17	2,090	10.63	12.25
15- 19.9	103,468	7.99	1,802	9.17	17.42
20- 29.9	106,399	8.22	2,589	13.17	24.33
30- 49.9	80,333	6.20	3,053	15.54	38.01
50- 69.9	28,094	2.17	1,646	8.38	58.59
70- 99.9	17,029	1.31	1,408	7.16	82.61
100-149.9	9,349	0.72	1,124	5.71	120.21
150-199.9	3,146	0.24	514	2.76	171.97
200-299.9	2,587	0.20	623	3.17	240.95
300-499.9	1,368	0.11	518	2.63	378.40
500-999.9	674	0.05	453	2.30	671.87
>1,000	196	0.02	344	1.75	1,752.60
Totals	1,295,001	100.00	19,650	100.00	15.17

Source: National Land Commission, Ch'uan-kuo t'u-ti tiao-ch'a pao-kao kang-yao [Preliminary report of the national land survey] (Nanking, 1937), p. 33.

Note: The provinces included are Chahar, Suiyuan, Shensi, Shansi, Hopei, Shantung, Honan, Kiangsu, Anhwei, Chekiang, Hupei, Hunan, Kiangsi, Fukien, Kwangtung, Kwangsi.

whom attained their initial wealth from sources other than farming. In other words, land was a possible object of investment by rich merchants and others in those parts of China where rates of return were reasonable because well-established markets for grain served by inexpensive water transport existed, namely, in the more urbanized and commercialized Yangtze Valley and in the south.[78] The data in table 16(5) show a rough correlation between rents as a percentage of land value and the incidence of tenancy in the several provinces. Kweichow is something of an anomaly in the southwest, as is Shantung in the north. In the former case, as perhaps in other relatively poor and backward areas, the basis for high rates of tenancy may have lain in the persistence of "feudal" landlord-tenant relations (labor services, miscellaneous exactions, tighter controls) rather than in the strictly commercial return on the land.[79] High returns to land ownership in Shantung where the overall tenancy rate was low I am for the moment unable to explain; the problem may result from the figure chosen by the National Agricultural Research Bureau's investigators for the "average" value of a mou of land in Shantung.[80]

Estimates of the extent of tenancy in republican China vary considerably, and of course local differences were enormous, but overall about 50 percent of the peasantry were involved in the landlord-tenant relationship--about 30 percent as tenants who rented all of the land that that they farmed, and 20 percent more as owner-tenants who rented part of their land. Table 16(1) presents two estimates of the rates of tenancy by province in the 1930s, which--although they differ in detail--indicate clearly the much greater incidence of pure tenancy in the rice-growing provinces of the Yangtze Valley and the southern coast than in the wheat-growing north.[81] These provincial data obscure the often very considerable local variations within any province resulting from location, land quality, degree of commercialization, and historical accretions.[82] It should also be noted that the categories owner, owner-tenant, and tenant do not necessarily represent a descending order of economic well-being. The somewhat more complex categorization of the National Land Commission's 1934-1935 survey shown in table 17, for example, is a warning that the rubric "owner-tenant" in table 16(1) subsumes every case from a landlord who rents 1 percent of his land to a poor peasant who rents 99 percent. The farmers of Shansi, Shantung, Hopei, and Honan, predominantly owner-cultivators with lesser population pressure and larger farms, were not better off with respect to family income than their tenant brethren in Kwangtung. Nor is tenancy incompatible with economic progress: note that in the United States the percentage of farm operators who were tenants increased from 25.6 percent in 1879 to 34.5 percent in 1945.

TABLE 16, PART 1

TENANCY, RENTED LAND, FARM SIZE, RENT SYSTEMS, AND RENTAL RATES IN THE 1930s
(Twenty-two Provinces, Excluding Manchuria)

Province	(1) Percentage of Farm Families (Hu) Who Are Owners, Owner-Tenants, Tenants						
	NARB, 1931-1936 Average				Buck, 1929-1933		
	No. hsien Reporting 1936	Owner	Owner-Tenant	Tenant	No. Localities Surveyed	Owner	Owner-Tenant	Tenant
Northwest								
Chahar	(10)	39	26	35	--	--	--	--
Suiyuan	(13)	56	18	26	--	--	--	--
Ninghsia	(5)	62	11	27	(1)	96	1	3
Tsinghai	(8)	55	24	21	(2)	20	8	72
Kansu	(29)	59	19	22	(6)	58	16	26
Shensi	(49)	55	22	23	(20)	68	15	17
North								
Shansi	(90)	62	21	17	(4)	38	38	24
Hopei	(126)	68	20	12	(6)	71	17	12
Shantung	(100)	71	17	12	(15)	72	18	10
Honan	(89)	56	22	22	(8)	58	23	19
East								
Kiangsu	(56)	41	26	33	(6)	31	23	46
Anhwei	(41)	34	22	44	(2)	35	13	52
Chekiang	(62)	21	32	47	(14)	29	20	51
Central								
Hupei	(48)	31	29	40	(5)	35	31	34
Hunan	(41)	25	27	48	(13)	16	27	57
Kiangsi	(57)	28	31	41	(7)	33	35	32
Southeast								
Fukien	(42)	26	32	42	(1)	30	55	15
Kwangtung	(55)	21	27	52	(13)	16	35	49
Kwangsi	(50)	33	27	40	--	--	--	--
Southwest								
Kweichow	(23)	32	25	43	(6)	25	22	53
Yunnan	(39)	34	28	38	(8)	49	27	24
Szechwan	(87)	24	20	56	(3)	27	15	58
National average (excluding Manchuria)	(1,120)	46	24	30	(146)	44	23	33

Sources: (1) Nung-ch'ing pao-kao, 5.12 (December 1937), p. 330, in Chang Yu-i, Chung-kuo chin-tai nung-yeh shih tzu-liao, vol. 3, pp. 728-730. Buck, Statistics, pp. 57-59.

TABLE 16, PART 2

TENANCY, RENTED LAND, FARM SIZE, RENT SYSTEMS,
AND RENTAL RATES IN THE 1930s
(Twenty-two Provinces, Excluding Manchuria)

Province	(2) Rented Land as Percent Farm Area		(3) Percentage Distribution of Size of Farms Operated, 1934-1935 (mou)				
	National Land Commission	Buck	<10	10-29.9	30-49.9	50-99.9	>100
Northwest							
Chahar	10.2	---	1.4	7.9	2.2	8.9	79.6
Suiyuan	8.7	5.0	9.3	33.3	16.2	18.4	22.8
Ninghsia	---	0.5	---	---	---	---	---
Tsinghai	---	9.5	---	---	---	---	---
Kansu	---	9.1	---	---	---	---	---
Shensi	16.6	17.4	38.7	35.9	12.8	10.1	2.5
North							
Shansi	---	15.8	16.9	41.0	20.3	16.1	5.7
Hopei	12.9	9.8	40.0	41.4	10.8	6.1	1.7
Shantung	12.6	9.8	49.7	38.5	7.9	3.3	0.6
Honan	27.3	19.7	47.9	34.6	9.5	6.2	1.8
East							
Kiangsu	42.3	33.3	52.3	38.1	5.8	2.5	1.3
Anhwei	52.6	51.0	47.0	38.2	9.6	4.5	0.7
Chekiang	51.3	31.0	67.0	27.8	3.5	1.4	0.3
Central							
Hupei	27.9	31.2	60.4	32.0	5.5	1.8	0.2
Hunan	47.8	36.6	56.5	33.4	6.3	3.1	0.8
Kiangsi	45.1	51.4	54.2	41.6	3.7	0.5	*
Southeast							
Fukien	39.3	55.7	71.8	24.8	2.5	0.8	0.1
Kwangtung	76.9	59.6	87.4	12.3	0.3	*	---
Kwangsi	21.2	26.0	51.1	37.7	7.2	3.0	0.9
Southwest							
Kweichow	---	25.8	---	---	---	---	---
Yunnan	---	27.6	---	---	---	---	---
Szechwan	---	52.4	---	---	---	---	---
National average (excluding Manchuria)	30.7	28.7	47.0	32.4	7.8	5.4	7.4

Sources: (2) Buck, Statistics, pp. 55-56. National Land Commission, Ch'uan-kuo t'u-ti tiao-ch'a pao-kao kang-yao, p. 37. (3) Ch'uan-kuo t'u-ti tiao-ch'a pao-kao kang-yao, pp. 26-27.

* Less than 0.05%.

TABLE 16, PART 3

TENANCY, RENTED LAND, FARM SIZE, RENT SYSTEMS, AND RENTAL RATES IN THE 1930s
(Twenty-two Provinces, Excluding Manchuria)

	(4)			(5)			
	Percentage Distribution of Types of Rent, 1934			Rents as a Percentage of Land Values, 1934			
Province	Cash	Fixed Kind (Crop)	Share	Cash	Fixed Kind (Crop)	Share	Fixed Kind and Share Rents as a Percentage of Value of Crop, 1931
Northwest							
Chahar	19	51	30	2.9	4.4	6.9	37.5
Suiyuan	31	23	46	6.4	14.4	12.0	---
Ninghsia	46	19	35	---	---	---	⎱ 30.9
Tsinghai	11	54	35	---	---	---	⎰
Kansu	14	51	35	11.4	12.0	13.7	
Shensi	15	9	26	10.1	13.0	12.6	41.1
North							
Shansi	27	45	27	6.2	5.9	6.2	50.1
Hopei	52	22	26	7.3	7.6	8.1	49.1
Shantung	30	31	39	16.0	18.8	20.8	46.5
Honan	17	39	44	---	---	---	49.5
East							
Kiangsu	28	53	19	8.7	7.8	12.8	40.3
Anhwei	14	53	33	9.4	9.4	16.4	40.4
Chekiang	27	66	7	9.6	10.3	13.2	42.4
Central							
Hupei	20	58	22	8.3	6.8	13.6	38.6
Hunan	0	74	18	17.4	17.4	28.5	44.2
Kiangsi	7	80	13	19.2	18.1	36.8	42.6
Southeast							
Fukien	19	56	25	17.8	19.9	21.0	44.7
Kwangtung	24	58	18	17.0	19.0	15.4	42.5
Kwangsi	6	65	29	---	---	---	43.1
Southwest							
Kweichow	10	40	50	6.2	13.4	12.1	51.4
Yunnan	14	61	25	13.9	16.6	16.8	43.4
Szechwan	26	58	16	11.4	14.5	16.9	49.1
National average (excluding Manchuria)	21	51	28	11.0	12.9	14.1	43.3

Sources: (4) Nung-ch'ing pao-kao, 3.4 (April 1935), p. 90, in National Government, Directorate of Statistics, Chung-kuo tsu-tien chih-tu chih t'ung-chi fen-hsi [Statistical analysis of China's land rent system] (Shanghai: Chengchung, 1946), p. 43. (5) Nung-ch'ing pao-kao, 3.6 (June 1935), in Chung-kuo tsu tien chih-tu chih t'ung-chi fen-hsi, p. 79. Ch'en Cheng-mo, Chung-kuo ko-sheng ti ti-tsu [Land rents in China by province] (Shanghai: Commercial Press, 1936), pp. 94-95.

TABLE 17

PERCENTAGE OF FARM FAMILIES
IN VARIOUS OWNERSHIP CATEGORIES
(1,745,344 Families in 16 Provinces, 1934-1935)

Landlord	2.05
Landlord-owner	3.15
Landlord-owner-tenant	0.47
Landlord-tenant	0.11
Owner	47.61
Owner-tenant	20.81
Tenant	15.78
Tenant-laborer	0.02
Laborer	1.57
Other	8.43

Source: Ch'uan-kuo t'u-ti tiao-ch'a pao-kao
kang-yao, p. 35.

Reliable historical data on the changing incidence of tenancy are nearly nonexistent. A comparison of the estimates compiled in the 1880s by local observers, missionaries and others with those compiled for the 1930s suggests considerable variation up and down by locality but no significant change in the overall tenancy rate. [83] National Agricultural Bureau estimates show only a slight change (farmers who rented all of their land increased from 28 percent in 1912 to 30 percent of farm families in 1931-1936), which is probably not significant since the 1931-1935 data were obtained from regular mail questionnaires completed by thousands of volunteer crop reporters--many of whom were rural school teachers--while those for 1912 were a conjecture only. [84] Myers' comparison of twenty-two hsien in Shantung in the 1890s and 1930s finds that the percentage of tenant households fell in thirteen and rose in nine hsien. [85] Comparative data from Honan, Anhwei, Kiangsi, and Hupei for 1913, 1923, and 1934 show no significant changes: tenants increased from 39 to 41 percent and owner-tenants from 27 to 28 percent, while owner-cultivators declined from 34 to 31 percent. [86]

The relatively slow rise of land values as compared with other prices shown in table 14 may imply that the demand for land was comparatively weak in the relatively unsettled circumstances of the 1920s when, as Buck observed, "agitation against landlords . . . reduced the demand for land and even encouraged owners to sell their property."[87] Finally, as I have indicated above, the amount of cultivated land distributed during land reform in the first years of the People's Republic-- even after a dozen very bad years of war and civil war--was approximately the same as that controlled by landlords in the mid-1930s. One may perhaps conclude that while land was regularly bought and sold, the basic pattern of high tenancy in some areas and low tenancy in others-- based primarily on the differential economic return to landlords, but also on the persistence of "extra-economic" labor service and other exactions in the most backward areas--was not significantly altered in the republican era.

Was the tenant's position secure? Overall, it may have become slightly less so in the course of the twentieth century. A rough comparison of ninety-three hsien in eight provinces between 1924 and 1934 shows a small increase in the percentage of annual rentals, no change in three to ten year contracts, and slight decreases in ten to twenty year and permanent rentals. [88] That the 1930 Land Law, for example, contained a provision to the effect that the tenant had the right to extend his lease indefinitely unless the landlord took the land back at the expiration of the contract and farmed it himself, indicates recognition of the problem of insecure peasant holdings. No effort was made to enforce the law; hence insecurity of tenure undoubtedly continued to be a problem. As part of the process of modernization of property concepts in rural China, the system of "permanent tenancy" (yung-t'ien) which had sharply differentiated the tenant's ownership of a "surface right" from the landlord's "bottom right" was gradually disappearing. Permanent tenure was replaced by less permanent contracts. The insecurity of the annual contract put the peasant at a considerable disadvantage and allowed the landlord to impose additional burdens in the form of rent deposits (as security against nonpayment of rents) and higher rents.

But these trends were occurring only very slowly. Of greater immediate significance for the productivity of China's agriculture is the continuing positive correlation in the eight provinces referred to above between the incidence of longer rent contracts, including permanent tenure, and the percentage of tenancy. The National Land Commission's 1934-1935 survey also found yung-t'ien to be most prevalent in Kiangsu, Anhwei, and Chekiang--three provinces with high tenancy rates.[89] While tenants would have had an even greater incentive to improve their land if they had owned it outright, the long-run economic interests of both tenant and landlord appear to have resulted in sufficiently long rental contracts--on the average, of course, local conditions varied enormously--in areas of high tenancy so that tenant incentives to increase productivity by investing in the land they farmed were not completely discouraged.

A 1932 survey of 849 hsien by the Ministry of the Interior found that the rent deposit system (ya-tsu) was prevalent in 220 hsien (26 percent) and present in 60 others.[90] Land rents were paid in three principal forms: cash, crop, and share rent. The National Agricultural Research Bureau's 1934 survey reported that 50.7 percent of tenants paid a fixed amount of their principal crops, 28.1 percent were sharecroppers, and 21.2 percent paid a fixed cash rent (see table 16(4)). Comparable data in the 1934-1935 land survey were: crop rent, 60.01 percent of tenants; cash rent, 24.62 percent; share rent, 14.99 percent; labor rent, 0.24 percent; and others, 0.14 percent.[91] The incidence of cash rent was perhaps increasing very slowly in the twentieth century.[92]

In general, as shown in table 16(5), the burden of share rent (which depended upon the extent to which the landlord provided seeds, tools, and draft animals, and which averaged 14.1 percent of land value according to the National Agricultural Research Bureau) was slightly greater than crop rent (12.9 percent), and crop rent was greater than cash rent (11.0 percent). Rents in kind, fixed and share, averaged 43.3 percent of the value of the main crop when the tenant supplied seeds, fertilizer, and draft animals. The failure of the Kuomintang policy of limiting rents to 37.5 percent of the main crops is evident. In whatever form they were paid, rents were considerably higher, in absolute terms and in relation to the value of the land, in south China than they were in the north--but so too was the output per mou of land. A fixed rent in kind was the dominant system except for north China and Kweichow in the southwest, accounting for 62 percent of rental arrangements in the five provinces with the highest incidence of tenancy (Anhwei, Chekiang, Hunan, Kwangtung, and Szechwan--I omit Kweichow whose circumstances as suggested above require a different analysis), and only 39 percent in the five provinces with the lowest tenancy rates (Shensi, Shansi, Hopei, Shantung, and Honan). Under this arrangement, a tenant paid his landlord a fixed amount of grain whether he had a good harvest or bad--with possibly a reduction or postponement in catastrophically bad years. When combined with longer-term contracts, which were also more common in the high tenancy rice-growing provinces, a fixed rent in kind permitted the tenant to benefit from improvements in productivity resulting from his labor and investment and thus provided a greater incentive for increased output than did sharecropping. Share rents were more common (32 percent) in the five low tenancy north China provinces, where security of tenure was also less, than they were in the five high tenancy provinces (18 percent). Contract terms were thus less encouraging to peasant investment in land improvements in the north than in the south, but tenancy was also less prevalent in the north.

Neither the fate of individual tenant families, nor the rich variety of local practices, nor the limits within which increased output could be furthered (given other technological, financial, and organizational constraints) by these apparently rational aspects of the tenancy system have been adequately dealt with by the province-level quantitative treatment that I have offered. To what degree real peasant tenants in specific areas at specific times realized sufficient family income to make improvements which increased their total output can only be determined by detailed local studies such as those by Myers of Hopei and Shantung and by Ash of Kiangsu, with the former finding positively and the latter negatively. Data such as those which appear in table 16 may have limited reliability as absolute values, although they are probably good enough to reflect the broad outlines of the tenancy system and its conditions. Again they suggest the real but limited growth potentialities of traditional agricultural arrangements--so long as population growth was held down by Malthusian controls, and so long as the population would accept a constant but low standard of living.

The patterns of land tenure and cultivation described above were intimately connected with the structure of credit, marketing, and taxation as these related to agriculture. Agriculture being an industry of slow turnover, the small peasant in China, as in other countries, was often unable to survive the interval between sowing and harvesting without borrowing. The pervasiveness and burden of rural indebtedness were a major source of rural discontent. Buck reports that 39 percent of the farms surveyed in 1929-1933 were in debt. The National Agricultural Research Bureau estimated that, in 1933, 56 percent of farms had borrowed cash and 48 percent had borrowed grain for food. A third national estimate noted that 43.87 percent of farm families were in debt in 1935. [93] All observers agree that overwhelmingly the rural debt had been incurred to meet household consumption needs rather than for investment in production and that for the poorer peasants indebtedness

was the rule. [94] Interest rates were high--a reflection of the desperate
need of the peasant, the shortage of capital in rural China, the risk of
default, and the absence of either government or cooperative alternative
modern lending facilities. On small loans in kind, an annual rate of
100 to 200 percent might be charged. The bulk of peasant loans, perhaps two-thirds, paid annual rates of 20 to 40 percent; about one-tenth
paid less than 20 percent; and the rest, more than 40 percent. About
two-thirds of all loans were for periods of six months to one year. [95]
Agricultural credit came largely from individuals--landlords, wealthier
farmers, merchants--as the 1934 data in table 18 indicate.

There were few modern banks (government or private) to be found
in rural areas, and in any case such banks did not invest in consumption
loans. The seven modern banks in Kiangsi, to give an example, had
only 0.078 percent of their outstanding loan funds in 1932 invested in
farm loans. [96] Considerable attention has been directed to the rural
cooperative movement which began in the 1920s, but even at their peak
the cooperatives never involved more than a tiny fraction of Chinese
farmers. [97] The moneylender, who was often the landlord or the grain
merchant, performed the function of transferring part of the surplus

TABLE 18

SOURCES OF FARM CREDIT, 1934

Source of Farm Credit	Percentage of Total Number of Loans
Banks	2.4
Cooperatives	2.6
Pawnshops	8.8
Native banks	5.5
Village stores and shops	13.1
Landlords	24.2
Well-to-do farmers	18.4
Merchants	25.0

Source: National Agricultural Research Bureau, Crop
Reporting in China, 1934 (Nanking, 1936), p. 70.

of agriculture back to the peasant--thus allowing him to live beyond his means, but at the ultimate cost of preserving intact a landlord dominated rural society.

The Chinese village was not economically self-sufficient, although a larger unit, Skinner's "standard marketing area," can be considered for many purposes to have been self-sufficient. To meet cash obligations such as rent and taxes, and to purchase many necessities, some part of the farmer's crop had to be disposed of on the market. About 15 percent of the rice crop and 29 percent of the wheat crop were sold by the peasants covered in Buck's survey, while the proportion for cash crops such as tobacco, opium, peanuts, rapeseed, and cotton was, of course, considerably higher. [98] In many cases the peasant had no choice but to sell in the local market. He was separated from more distant markets not only by inadequate and thus costly transportation, but perhaps also by an information barrier--although the burden of rural illiteracy has probably been exaggerated. The market was subject to considerable price fluctuations, which might be unfavorable to the peasant as a result of the fact that supply would naturally be larger at harvest time when he wanted to sell and smaller in the spring when he wanted to buy. Moreover, in those areas near the major cities in eastern and southern coastal China where the commercialization of agriculture had made some headway, exploitative collection systems (such as that operated by the British and American Tobacco Company) put the farmer at the mercy of the buyer.

While as a small individual buyer and seller the peasant was unable to influence the markets in which he had to trade, to imply in crude Marxist (and Confucian) terms that all merchants were parasites who contributed nothing to the economy or to suggest that increased commercialization of agriculture in the twentieth century had a negative effect on rural production and income is absurd. In the atomistic rural sector--where there were no barriers to entry (other than the often exaggerated information barrier), virtually no government intervention, and low capital requirements for all businesses--most types of commerce were quite competitive. High profits quickly lured new entrants into existing markets. The richest merchants (who, in China, as elsewhere, did business in the more commercialized areas where almost everyone was informed, mobile, and experienced in dealing with markets) made their profits not by fleecing their customers, but by specialization, division of labor, and offering critical services at low unit prices. The local market has frequently been described as tending to monopsony for what the peasant sold and to monopoly for what he bought, but in fact there have been few studies to document this common assumption. If more than two-thirds of marketed crops were sold locally (as Perkins suggests; see page 48 above), then this trade may have involved few merchants at all--periodic markets were places where farmers bought from and sold to each other. If Perkins is also right that most rice marketings were by landlords (see pages 54-56 above) who did not have to sell at harvest time and who had the information and connections which made it difficult to fleece them, then there is little support for monopsony.

I have noted above that the terms of trade between agriculture and industry were generally favorable to the farmer before 1931. The ability to grow and market cash crops was a major factor supporting the modest increase in total agricultural output which occurred between 1912 and the 1930s and which kept per capita rural incomes roughly constant over this period. That the agricultural market was fragmented, sometimes appearing to be stacked against the small peasant producer, and perhaps burdened with excessive middlemen, prevented greater increases in output and clearly detracted from rural welfare. But it did function well enough before 1937 to help keep the traditional economic system afloat.

Under both the Peking government until 1927 and the Nanking government which followed, agricultural taxation was probably inequitable in incidence, but the matter has never been carefully studied. The land tax was largely a provincial or local levy. Collusion between the local elite and the tax collector was common, with the result that a disproportionate share of the burden fell upon the small owner-farmer. Land taxes were also shifted onto tenants in the form of higher rents. Such additional abuses as forced collections in advance, the manipulation of exchange rates, and multiple surcharges were also reported.[99] In the last decade of Kuomintang rule, the tax burden on the small owner and the tenant was increased by wartime tax collection in kind and compulsory grain purchases by the Chungking government.

If the incidence was inequitable, the most important economic characteristic of the pre-1949 land tax was its failure to recover a major share of the agricultural surplus appropriated by the landlord for redistribution to productive investment. The level of taxation in fact was low, reflecting the superficial penetration of the state into local society (see page 76 below). As in the cases of credit and marketing, the system of agricultural taxation reinforced a pattern of income distribution which allowed only a very modest overall growth of output with no increase at all in individual income and welfare.

Quantitative treatment of the fate of China's agriculture between 1937 and 1949 is nearly impossible. War and civil war put an end to even the modest collection of rural statistical data of the Nanking government decade. The principal scene of fighting was north China, and it is certain that physical damage to agricultural land, transportation disruptions, conscription of manpower and draft animals, requisitions of grain for the armies, and mounting political conflict affected farmers in the north much more severely than in south and west China.[100] The prewar process of increasing commercialization was reversed, agricultural productivity and output declined, and commodity trade between rural and urban areas was disrupted. Even by 1950, according to rural surveys made in the first two years of the People's Republic, some areas in north China--because of manpower and draft animal losses-- had not returned to their peak prewar output levels.[101] Both the harsh Japanese occupation and the great battles of 1948-1949 left the south and west relatively unscathed, but here too manpower and grain requisitions by the military took their toll, and runaway inflation from 1947 undermined the supply of foodstuffs and industrial crops to the urban areas. The collapse of both the rural and the urban economies of China was a fact by mid-1948.

VII. Transportation

Poorly developed transportation continued to be a major shortcoming of the Chinese economy throughout the republican period. This is apparent at both the microscopic and macroscopic levels. In 1919, the cost of production of a ton of pig iron at the Hanyang Ironworks in Hupei, China's major producer, was Ch$ 48.50 while in 1915 the Japanese ironworks at Pen-ch'i in Manchuria produced pig iron at Ch$ 22.00 per ton. As compared with a cost of Ch$ 5.74 a ton for coke produced locally at Pen-ch'i, high transportation charges attributable to slow progress in building the Canton-Hankow railroad and inefficient handling by native boats of the water portion of the trip from P'inghsiang in Kiangsi 300 miles away forced up the cost of coke at Hanyang to Ch$ 24.54 a ton.[102] Since both firms obtained their raw materials from their own "captive" mines, it is not likely that the difference was due to market fluctuations between the two dates.

The wages of coolie labor were incredibly low, but the economic efficiency of the human carriers who dominated transportation at the local level was even lower. One observer reported:

On the road from the Wei Basin to the Chengtu Plain,

in Szechuan Province, one may meet coolies carrying
on their backs loads of cotton weighing 160 pounds.
They will carry these loads fifteen miles a day for 750
miles at a rate of seventeen cents (Mexican) a day,
which is the equivalent of fourteen cents a ton mile.
At this rate it costs $ 106.25 to transport one ton 750
miles. The railways should be able to haul this for
$ 15, or one seventh the amount. The Peking-Mukden
Railway carries coal for the Kailan Mining Company at
less than 1 1/2 cents a ton mile. With the coolie carriers the cotton spends fifty days on the road, whereas
the railway would make the haul in two days, thereby
saving forty-eight days interest on the money and land-
ing the cotton in better condition.[103]

Comparative costs of transportation in China by the principal
modes of conveyance have been estimated (Chinese cents per ton-
kilometer) as follows: junks, 2 to 12; steamers and launches, 2 to 15;
railroads, 3.2 to 17; carts, 5 to 16.5; wheelbarrows, 10 to 14; camels,
10 to 20; motor trucks, 10 to 56; donkeys, mules and horses, 13.3 to
25; human porterage, 14 to 50; and rickshaw, 20 to 35.[104] Throughout
the republican era, the bulk of goods continued to be carried by traditional means of transportation. The data for 1933, for example, which
was not an atypical year, show that old-fashioned transportation contributed three times as much (Ch$ 1.2 billion) to national income as did
modern transportation (Ch$ 430 million).

An adequate railroad network would have greatly reduced transport costs and facilitated the development of the interior. Among other
things, goods carried by rail more often escaped likin and other local
transit duties. The presence of a railroad also tends to standardize
weights and measures and currency along the line. However, the example of British India should make it evident that a great railway network can coexist with a backward agricultural economy, and that mere
length of railroad mileage does not lead automatically to economic
development. In any case, the railroads of republican China were inadequate in length, distribution, and operation. At the end of World
War II, China, including Manchuria and Taiwan, had a total of 24,945
kilometers of main and branch railroad lines.[105] The amount built in
each of the periods into which we may conventionally divide the republican era was as follows:

Before 1912	9, 618.10 kms
1912-1927	3, 422.38
1928-1937	7, 895.66
1938-1945	3, 909.38
Total	24, 945.52 kms

While the first railroad in China (an unauthorized fifteen kilometer line running from Woosung to Shanghai built by Jardine, Matheson and Company and other foreigners) was opened in 1876 local antipathy was so violent that this line was purchased and scrapped by the Chinese government. Continued opposition from both the local population and conservative officials prevented any progress with railroad construction until China's defeat by Japan in 1894-1895 altered the situation. On the one hand, the "self-strengtheners" were able to convince the court of the necessity to build railroads as a means of bolstering the dynasty against further foreign incursions. On the other hand, the exposure of China's weakness attracted foreign capital which saw the financing of railroad construction as a means to promote foreign political influence and economic penetration. Only 364 kilometers of track had been laid by 1894. In the first great wave of railroad building, between 1895 and 1911, 9, 253 kilometers of line were completed, for the most part with funds borrowed from foreign creditors. Of this total, the Russian-built Chinese Eastern Railway across Manchuria and its southern extension from Harbin to Dairen accounted for 2, 425 kilometers.

The failure of private railroad projects undertaken by provincial gentry and merchants in the last decade of the Manchu dynasty inspired the railroad nationalization program which was an immediate cause of the overthrow of the dynasty. In the era of Yuan Shih-k'ai and the warlord regimes which followed until 1927, railroad construction slowed down perceptibly. The several private lines were nationalized without the violent opposition which had been fatal to the Ch'ing dynasty, and for the most part in exchange for government bonds that were soon in default. While new loans were arranged with foreign lenders and some pre-1912 loans renegotiated, World War I put a halt to European investment in Chinese railroads. When a new Four-Power Consortium was put together in 1920, the Peking government, contrary to American expectations, refused to do business with it. Construction within China proper was limited to the completion of the Peking-Suiyuan line, and of sections of the Canton-Hankow and Lunghai railroads, altogether totalling about 1, 700 kilometers. An equal amount of new track was built in Manchuria, consisting on the one hand of Japanese financed feeder lines to the South Manchurian Railway and, on the other hand, of rival lines built by Chang Tso-lin in part with funds obtained from the revenue of the Peking-Mukden railroad. Both the Chinese construction in north China and the new Manchurian lines were motivated as much by strategic as by economic considerations.

Between 1928 and 1937, approximately 3,400 kilometers of railroad were constructed within China proper, including the completion of the Canton-Hankow line, the Chekiang-Kiangsi railroad, and the Tungpu line in Shansi. This task was achieved without major foreign borrowing: the Chekiang-Kiangsi railroad, for example, was financed mainly by loans from the Bank of China, and the Shansi railroad was financed out of provincial revenues. As in other areas, however, the demands of military spending and debt service left very little funds for the economic "reconstruction" about which the Nanking government talked so much. In the same period, some 4,500 kilometers of railroad were built in Manchuria, consisting mainly of new Japanese construction after 1931 as part of the planned development of Manchukuo into an industrial base. In spite of formidable obstacles during the Sino-Japanese war, the Chinese government claimed to have completed in unoccupied China some 1,500 kilometers of railroad lines which played an important part in supporting the economy and military effort. The Japanese, for their part, constructed a number of additional lines in Manchuria.

Of the railways built by 1937, approximately 42 percent of the total track was located in Manchuria, 32 percent in China proper north of the Yangtze River, 22 percent in south China, and 4 percent in Taiwan. The relatively small railroad mileage in densely populated south China in part of course testifies to the persistence of an elaborate premodern (junk and sampan) and modern (steamboat and steam launch) network of water transportation which continued to compete effectively with the steam train. In proportion to area and population, Manchuria was far better served than any other region in China, a circumstance underlying and reflecting Manchuria's more extensive industrialization. No railroad had penetrated to the rich province of Szechwan or to such western areas as Kansu, Sinkiang, and Tibet. Apart from the notoriously small total mileage in relation to the size of the country, the development of China's railroads had been quite haphazard, and the distribution of lines was often uneconomic. For China proper a more desirable system might have been a radial network centering perhaps at Hankow. The actual system was a parallel network heavily concentrated in northern and eastern China. In Manchuria, a combined radial-parallel network had

developed which was marred by the uneconomic duplication of lines resulting from Chinese-Japanese competition in the northeast in the 1920s.

The construction of the Chinese railway system had involved considerable borrowing from Great Britain, Belgium, Japan, Germany,
France, the United States, and the Netherlands--in order of the total
amount of loans extended by each country from 1898 to 1937. These
loans (the terms of which often involved de facto foreign control of the
lines constructed) were concentrated in the last years of the Ch'ing
dynasty and first decade of the republic, and reflected the scramble for
railroad concessions and loan contracts by foreign syndicates whose
rivalry and intrigues were as much political as financial. Repayment
of the railroad debt was to come from the operating revenue of the lines,
but from about 1925 to 1935 most of the foreign railroad loans were in
default. On December 31, 1935, the total outstanding indebtedness, including principal and interest in arrears, amounted to approximately
£ 53,827,443 or Ch$ 891,920,730.[106] Railroad bonds had fallen to as
little as 11 percent of their face value in the case of the Lunghai railroad.

The earning power of the Chinese Government Railways was potentially just sufficient to pay the interest due to bondholders. Annual net
operating revenue during 1916-1939 averaged 7.4 percent of the cost of
road and equipment while interest rates on railroad loans ranged from
5 to 8 percent. That is, while their operation was apparently less efficient than that of the South Manchurian Railway, the government railroads were economically viable enterprises which both contributed to
such economic growth as the republican years saw and generally produced a small profit. On the average, however, only 35 percent of the
net operating revenue in these two decades was allocated to interest
payments. Large portions of the net operating revenue--more than 50
percent, for example, in the years 1926, 1927, and 1930-1934--were
remitted to the Chinese government which utilized these funds for its
general expenditures.[107] Remittances to the government during 1921-
1936 were double the amount appropriated for additions to railroad
equipment.

A principal cause of the low profitability of the Chinese Government Railways was the prolonged civil strife throughout the republic.
Rival warlords not only commandeered railroad lines for troop transportation, but at times diverted passenger and freight revenues to the
maintenance of their armies. Twenty-one percent of the passenger
traffic (in passenger miles) carried on the Peking-Hankow railroad
between 1912 and 1925, for example, was military traffic; on the Peking-

Mukden line between 1920 and 1931, 17 percent of the passenger traffic was military.[108] Apart from direct war damage, which was perhaps minimal, repairs to the roadbed and rolling stock were neglected. For more than two decades the Ministry of Railways could rely regularly only on the income of a few lesser lines; and the system as a whole became increasingly obsolescent and inefficient. Table 19 shows the changes in the movement of passengers and freight over the Chinese Government Railways during 1912-1947.

Both passenger and freight traffic increased annually until the mid-1920s. The Northern Expedition and civil wars attendant upon the establishment of the Nanking regime affected both adversely, but in the relative calm of the 1930s railroad traffic revived and exceeded previous highs. Japanese seizure of the bulk of China's railways as the Nationalist government was forced into the interior between 1937 and 1945 is reflected in the figures for that period.

About 40 percent of the operating revenues of the Chinese Government Railways was realized from passenger service, of which a considerable part was troop movements. Minerals made up more than half of the freight carried; second in importance were agricultural products. The general pattern of freight traffic was one in which agricultural products and minerals were carried from inland points to the coastal treaty ports, while manufactured goods flowed into the interior. Increased transport of agricultural products in the first decade of the republic reflects the growth of cash crop output suggested in my discussion of agricultural trends above. The railroad in Manchuria in particular but also in north China facilitated the slow expansion of agricultural production shown in tables 12 and 13. Similarly, both the adverse effects of the depression on cash crop output and the recovery just prior to the outbreak of war in 1937 are evident in table 19.

Little need be said about motor road mileage apart from indicating that no improved roads suitable for motor vehicles existed in 1912. Before July 1937, about 116,000 kilometers of highways, of which 40,000 kilometers were surfaced, had been completed.[109] Most of this construction occurred after 1928, in which year there were perhaps 32,000 kilometers of highways, and was undertaken for military as much as commercial reasons by the Bureau of Public Roads of the National Economic Council. The "Seven Provinces Project," for example, in which Honan, Hupei, Anhwei, Kiangsi, Kiangsu, Chekiang, and Hunan cooperated, was conceived of as a means of tying together by a system of roads those provinces in which the Kuomintang government had its greatest strength. Sparse and primitive though they were, motor roads in 1937 tended to be better distributed within China proper than was the railroad network.

The war led to additional highway construction in the interior provinces, including, of course, the famous Yunnan-Burma highway. But in 1949 as in 1912, the great bulk of inland China continued to depend much more on traditional means of transportation, by water and land, for local and regional carriage than it did on motor vehicles or trains. By September 1941, for example, in the three provinces of Kiangsu, Chekiang, and Anhwei, 118,292 native boats (min-ch'uan), totalling 850,705 tons and with total crews of 459,178 persons, had registered with the boatman's associations established by the Wang Ching-wei government.[110] These boats were the principal means of short- and medium-distance bulk carriage in the lower Yangtze Valley and elsewhere in south and central China where a combination of rivers, lakes, and centuries' accumulation of man-made canals had produced a complex and extensive network of water transport. In contrast to local carriage, interport trade by the 1890s was already primarily carried by steamships, mainly foreign-owned. Nevertheless, the tonnage of Chinese junks entered and cleared by the Maritime Customs at the several treaty ports remained more or less constant from 1912 to 1922 and began to drop sharply only in the 1920s.[111] Steam shipping on China's major rivers increased steadily in the first decades of the twentieth century, as evidenced by the growth of registered tonnage of vessels under 1,000 tons from 42,577 in 1913 to 246,988 in 1933. Still, the river junk held its own in many places for a considerable period. Upriver from Ichang on the Yangtze, for example, junk tonnage increased slightly from the 1890s to 1917 before plunging downward in the 1920s. Between Nanning and Wuchow on the West River, junk traffic similarly gave way to steamships only in the 1920s.[112]

In the transportation sector, as in others we have discussed, the commonplace fact that China's economy changed only a little in the first half of the twentieth century has tended to be obscured, pushed out of sight by the disproportionate attention and space devoted to the small modern sector of the economy in official word and deed, in the writings of China's economists, in the yearbooks and reports intended for foreign consumption, and in the research which non-Chinese scholars--apart from the Japanese, who, in this matter, at least, had a more "realistic" view of China--have conducted on China's pre-1949 economy. For the Nanking government, which had abandoned the land and drew its revenues overwhelmingly from the modern sector, this building of paper castles reflected perhaps a deep, half-recognized desperation.

TABLE 19

INDEX NUMBERS OF PASSENGER MILES AND FREIGHT TON MILES CARRIED ON THE CHINESE GOVERNMENT RAILWAYS, 1912-1947

Year	(1912 = 100)		(1917 = 100)					
	Passenger Miles	Freight Ton Miles	Total Freight Ton Miles	Manufactures	Mineral Products	Agricultural Products	Forest Products	Animal Products
1912	100.0	100.0	---	---	---	---	---	---
1915	61.1	92.5	---	---	---	---	---	---
1916	127.2	107.7	94.7	94.8	93.8	91.3	81.0	126.9
1917	131.1	113.8	100.0	100.0	100.0	100.0	100.0	100.0
1918	143.0	140.8	123.8	124.6	127.6	123.5	120.9	97.8
1919	155.2	158.8	139.6	132.6	159.0	114.3	147.3	104.1
1920	194.8	186.7	164.1	138.2	165.0	186.2	171.6	102.3
1921	194.8	193.6	170.2	138.9	175.7	168.8	198.2	92.1
1922	204.6	163.7	143.9	155.7	151.4	127.8	188.8	127.7
1923	210.3	211.2	185.7	183.3	240.8	135.6	264.8	144.1
1924	220.7	187.9	165.2	157.5	199.4	102.7	226.1	121.5
1925	231.7	169.0	148.6	152.5	132.6	97.0	220.6	105.9
1926	159.9	99.6	---	---	---	---	---	---
1927	164.1	109.4	---	---	---	---	---	---
1928	144.8	96.0	---	---	---	---	---	---

Year									
1929	196.1	102.7	---	---	---	---	---	---	---
1931	267.4	183.3	161.1	217.0	165.3	104.2	151.6	113.9
1932	212.6	183.2	161.1	197.3	189.2	89.2	150.6	82.9
1933	248.3	196.1	172.4	200.9	192.4	94.6	146.3	89.3
1934-35	250.0	257.7	226.5	237.9	273.4	149.4	169.7	110.4
1935-36	267.9	266.8	234.5	268.3	282.6	152.9	152.0	122.3
1936-37	128.5	94.9	83.4	79.0	111.9	57.5	34.1	37.4
1937-38	56.3	51.4	45.2	22.0	22.9	87.1	44.3	18.2
1938-39	69.7	24.9	21.9	10.7	11.1	13.1	21.5	8.8
1939-40	88.6	20.5	18.0	9.9	8.3	10.7	9.7	7.3
1940-41	95.7	21.3	18.7	10.2	10.6	8.4	16.0	8.8
1941-42	90.7	19.1	16.8	8.7	10.0	9.1	14.2	4.9
1942-43	129.9	22.4	19.7	7.8	12.0	5.8	15.3	4.6
1943-44	62.1	9.4	8.3	3.1	5.7	1.8	10.5	1.6
1944-45	112.1	15.1	13.2	8.0	10.4	4.1	32.1	10.8
1945-46	765.1	154.4	135.8	83.2	80.0	54.3	249.1	89.5
1946-47	524.7	112.5	---	---	---	---	---	---

Source: Yen Chung-p'ing, Chung-kuo chin-tai ching-chi shih t'ung-chi tzu-liao hsuan-chi, pp. 207-208, 217.

VIII. Government and the Economy

Both the Peking warlords and a fortiori the Nanking regime which followed financed their governments primarily from the urban sector of the economy. Central government in republican China neither collected substantial revenue from the rural sector nor had very much influence over its collection and disbursal by semi-autonomous provincial and local interests. In other words, no national government before 1949 was able to channel a significant share of total national income through the central government treasury. As a result, government policies, while not without far-reaching consequences for the economy, were never realistically capable of pushing the Chinese economy forward on the path of modern economic growth.

During the years 1931-1936, for example, total national expenditures of the central government varied between a low of 2.1 percent and a high of 4.9 percent of the gross national product, and averaged 3.5 percent. (If the expenditures of all levels of local government were included, the percentage would perhaps be doubled.) Tax revenues were considerably less than this figure and reflected, on the one hand, the failure of the national government to mobilize the resources of the rural sector and, on the other, its inability or unwillingness to levy income taxes on society in general. Even this limited government revenue, moreover, was largely dissipated in maintaining a hypertrophic military establishment and financing continued civil war, or hypothecated to service the foreign and domestic debts. Neither the Peking nor the Nanking regime was able to finance any significant developmental investment out of its revenues, and the policies of neither were conducive to capital formation in the private sector of the economy.

Following the 1911 revolution, the new republican government at first struggled along with the Ch'ing fiscal system. While nomenclature and bureaucratic structure were soon changed, the republican government was even less able to control the revenue sources of China than its predecessor had been. In 1913, an effort was made to demarcate the sources of central, provincial, and local revenue, but the central government even under Yuan Shih-k'ai was too weak to enforce these regulations. After 1914, except for the Maritime Customs and the Salt Gabelle, the major taxes were administered by the provinces. Technically, the land tax (and several consumption taxes) still belonged to the central government, but in fact it was under provincial control and the proceeds were spent in and by the provinces, albeit under the accounting rubric "national expenditures of 'x' province." Yuan Shih-k'ai, until his death in 1916, was able to extract some land tax remittances from the provinces, and these continued fitfully and minimally until 1921, after which time the political situation so worsened and civil warfare became so widespread that Peking's financial control all but evaporated. [113]

Maritime Customs revenue was almost entirely committed to the service of foreign loans and indemnities. From 1912 through 1927 only Haikwan taels 142,341,000, or 20 percent, of a total revenue net of first charges of Haikwan taels 717,672,000 was available to the Peking government for administrative and other expenditures. [114] In spite of the revision of specific duties in 1902 and 1918, because of rising prices the actual rate of duty collected on imports hovered between 2.5 and 3.5 percent until 1923, when a further revision brought the effective duty to 5 percent. However, no major increase of revenue under this heading was possible until China regained tariff autonomy in 1930.

From 1913 through 1922, gross revenue from the Salt Gabelle exceeded gross Maritime Customs revenue. Especially after 1922, however, only a part of the income from salt was available to the central government. In order to furnish security for the Reorganization Loan of 1913, without which the government of Yuan Shih-k'ai might not have survived, a foreign Chief Inspector was appointed to supervise and in effect control the Salt Administration. While national pride might be hurt, this measure resulted in an immediate jump in the revenues collected on the account of the central government. Also, actual payments on foreign loans secured on the salt revenues were small--from 1917 the Reorganization Loan, for example, was paid from the Customs revenue. But this relatively happy situation was swept away by the continuous civil warfare. Provincial interference in the salt tax collection grew to serious proportions, salt funds were misappropriated, and smuggling increased. Total revenue fell markedly after 1922, as did the proportion of the collection that was actually remitted to Peking. Net collections, which had hit a peak of Ch$ 86 million in 1922, fell to Ch$ 71 million in 1924, Ch$ 64 million in 1926, and down to Ch$ 58 million in 1928. Even in 1922, only Ch$ 47 million (or 55 percent of the net collection) was actually remitted to Peking. Of the remaining amount, Ch$ 12 million was retained by the provinces with the central government's consent, but Ch$ 20 million (37 percent) was appropriated locally without consent. The total amount retained by provincial authorities and military commanders climbed to Ch$ 38 million in 1926, while the amount actually remitted to Peking in that year was barely Ch$ 9 million. [115]

Faced with a chronic state of financial embarrassment, the Peking government was forced to depend heavily on domestic and foreign borrowing. Between 1912 and 1926, twenty-seven domestic bond issues were floated by the Ministry of Finance with a combined face value of Ch$ 614 million. [116] Actual receipts to the government, however, were considerably smaller, for the bonds were always sold at a discount--as low as 20 percent of face value in an extreme case. A considerable amount of obscurity exists concerning the details of domestic loan flotations in this period, and on into the period of the Nanking government as well. There seems to have been a close relationship between the establishment of new banks with the right of note issue and government domestic borrowing. A large part of these issues was taken up by the Chinese "modern" banks who held government securities as investment and as reserves against note issue, as well as making direct advances to the government.

The Peking government transmitted a domestic indebtedness of only Ch$ 241 million to its successor, which would seem to indicate that its creditors, in spite of defaults, fared not too badly with the discounted Peking government bonds. Peking's domestic borrowing also permitted warlord coffers to be replenished time and again, although the proceeds of these loans brought little benefit to the economy of the country. Debt service on domestic and foreign loans, the largest single expenditure of the Peking government, together with military expenditure made up at least four-fifths of the total annual outlay. [117] After general administrative costs were met, there was nothing left for developmental investment. Provincial and local revenues, too, were drained by military and police outlays. [118] Nor were the foreign loans of the Peking regime usually undertaken with a view to furthering economic development.

New foreign loan obligations incurred in the period 1912-1926 were smaller in amount than the indemnity and railroad obligations of the last years of the Manchu dynasty. Total foreign holdings of Chinese government obligations (excluding the Boxer indemnity) increased from approximately US$ 526 million in 1913 to US$ 696 million in 1931. [119] The 1913 Reorganization Loan of £25 million was the largest single new foreign debt. A further significant part of this foreign borrowing was represented by the so-called "Nishihara loans" of 1918--unsecured advances by Japanese interests to the Anfu warlord clique then in power in Peking and to several provincial governments; the proceeds of these loans were used largely for civil war and political intrigue. Some of these advances were subsequently converted into legitimate railroad or telegraph loans, but the largest part, perhaps Ch$ 150 million, was never recognized by the Nanking government. Like the Japanese indemnity loans of the 1890s, Yuan Shih-k'ai's Reorganization Loan, and the domestic debt, this desperate borrowing by the Peking warlords contributed nothing, except for the several railroad loans, to the development of the Chinese economy. In fact, there is reason to believe that China annually made greater outpayments on account of government debt (including the Boxer indemnity) than she received in new loans. Remer, for example, estimates that annual outpayments averaged Ch$ 89.2 million during 1902-1913 and Ch$ 76.9 million during 1913-1930, while average inpayments in the two periods were Ch$ 61.0 million and Ch$ 23.8 million respectively. So large a "drain" of capital must be counted as a net withdrawal from China's economic resources, the effect of which was probably to handicap economic growth. [120]

The establishment of the Nanking government in 1928 nominally brought political unity after a decade of civil war. In the nine years from 1928-1937, the central government probably achieved a greater degree of fiscal control over China proper than had existed at any other time since the Ch'ing dynasty. Both revenues and the revenue system showed a remarkable improvement as compared with the warlord years of 1916-1927. Tariff autonomy was recovered in 1929-1930, and a new tariff with substantially higher rates gave a boost to the finances of the Kuomintang government. The shifting of import duties from a silver to a gold basis in 1930 through the instrumentality of Customs Gold Units both preserved the real value of customs revenue and provided increased yields in terms of falling silver, thus facilitating service of the large foreign and domestic debts. Salt revenue, which before 1928 was largely appropriated locally, was integrated into the national fiscal system. Transfers to the provinces continued, but a substantial part of the salt tax became effectively available to the central government. Many, although not all, of the numerous central and local excises were combined into a nationwide Consolidated Tax collected for the central government in exchange for provincial appropriation of the land tax revenue. Likin was substantially although not completely abolished. The currency system was unified with the virtual elimination of the tael in 1933 and the adoption in 1935 of a modern paper money system backed by foreign exchange reserves. This last was unintentionally facilitated by American silver purchases which drove up the price of silver and provided a substantial part of the required foreign currency reserves. In November 1935 silver was nationalized; the use of silver as currency forbidden; and the notes of the Central Bank of China, the Bank of China, and the Bank of Communications made full legal tender. The government experimented with an annual budget and greatly improved its collection and fiscal reporting services. Conferences were held and commissions appointed for the purpose of formulating and enforcing programs of fiscal reform and economic development. A National Economic Council was established in 1931 to direct the economic "reconstruction" of the country.

However impressive these accomplishments appeared at the time in contrast to what had gone before, they were still largely superficial ones. Based as it was on indirect taxation applied to the modern sectors of the economy, national government revenue was severely limited by the slow growth of output. The inability to tax agriculture placed a formidable constraint on potential tax revenues and thus on government programs. Customs, salt, and excise taxes probably bore heaviest on the small consumer, although the matter of the real incidence of taxation is a notably difficult one to trace; the well-to-do were not significantly taxed. The land tax in the hands of the provinces was neither reformed nor developed and likewise burdened the small peasant farmer disproportionately. The economic policies of the Kuomintang government did not cope with the fundamental problems of agriculture, did not promote industrial growth, and did not effectively harness the political and psychological support of the populace in an attempt to raise the Chinese economy out of its stagnation.[121] Whatever small gains had been made by 1937 were swept away by the war and civil war which filled the next twelve years and by the absence of governmental action to equalize in some measure the sacrifices which these years demanded of the Chinese people.

Table 20 shows the principal receipts and payments of the Nanking government for the nine fiscal years between 1928 and 1937. Some overall figures for the 1939-1948 period are also available, as will be seen below. Even when local government expenditures are added to those of the central government--local government expenditure remained important until 1938, declining rapidly thereafter in wartime in relation to central expenditure--the total constituted a very small proportion of China's gross national product, only 3.2 to 6 percent during 1931-1936. Comparable figures for the United States are 8.2 percent in 1929, 14.3 percent in 1933, and 19.7 percent in 1941.[122] The smallness of China's central government expenditures in relation to national income reflects both the narrowness of the national tax base and the limited size of the modern sector of the economy that in fact was called upon to shoulder the largest burden of national taxation.

Even into 1929 the Kuomintang government exercised some degree of fiscal control, apart from the Maritime Customs revenue, only in the five provinces of Chekiang, Kiangsu, Anhwei, Kiangsi, and Honan. This situation later improved, but complete central government dominance over north, northwest, and southwest China was never achieved before 1937. Soon after the outbreak of full-scale war, of course, the coastal and Yangtze provinces on which the government had principally based itself were lost to the Japanese. The demarcation of central and local revenues at a National Economic Conference in June 1928, by which the central government formally ceded the land tax to the provinces, was then less a policy aimed at improving the admittedly chaotic financial administration inherited from the Peking regime than it was a recognition of political reality by the Nanking government. It meant, however, that in return for tenuous political support, the central government of China abandoned any fiscal claim on that part of the economy which produced 65 percent of the national product. Abandoned too was any effort to overhaul an inequitable land tax system under which faulty land records and corrupt officials permitted the wealthy to escape a fair share of the burden. In consequence, a large part of the potential revenue of agriculture was withheld from community disposal for the general welfare.

In 1941, under the stress of war, the land-tax administration in unoccupied China was reclaimed from the provinces by the central government, which then granted cash subsidies to the local governments to compensate for their loss of revenue. Collection of the land tax in kind and the forced borrowing of grains which accompanied it provided 11.8 percent and 4.2 percent of the total central government revenue in 1942-1943 and 1943-1944. However, when the war with Japan ended, central government taxation of agricultural land was quickly dropped. Wartime collection of the land tax in kind did provide the central government with the greater measure of control over food supplies which it sought and, at the same time, dampened considerably the wartime rate of increase in note issue by reducing the government's direct outlay on foodstuffs needed to supply the army, civil servants, and city workers. It was carried out, however, without correcting any of the injustices of the antiquated land tax system, and individual small farmers were burdened with new inequities while other groups in the nation, for the most part, were exempted from or could avoid comparable direct taxation. [123]

Like almost all underdeveloped countries--Meiji Japan and post-1949 China are the major exceptions--the prewar Nanking government relied principally upon indirect taxation for its revenue: the three most important levies were customs duties (receipts from which rose rapidly after tariff autonomy was regained), the salt tax, and commodity taxes. As table 20 indicates, revenue under these three headings provided 55.7

TABLE 20

REPORTED RECEIPTS AND EXPENDITURES OF THE NANKING GOVERNMENT, 1928-1937
(Million Chinese $ and Percentage of Receipts and Expenditures)

	1928-1929		1929-1930		1930-1931		1931-1932		1932-1933	
	Ch$	%	Ch$	%	Ch$	%	Ch$	%	Ch$	%
Receipts [a]	434	100.0	585	100.0	774	100.0	749	100.0	699	100.0
Revenue [a]	334	77.0	484	82.7	557	72.0	619	82.6	614	87.8
Customs duty	179	41.2	276	47.2	313	40.4	357	47.7	326	46.6
Salt tax	30	6.9	122	20.8	150	19.4	144	19.2	158	22.6
Commodity taxes	33	7.6	47	8.0	62	8.0	96	12.8	89	12.7
Other [b]	92[c]	21.2	39	6.7	32	4.1	22	2.9	41	5.9
Deficit covered by borrowing	100	23.0	101	17.3	217	28.0	130	17.4	85	12.2
Expenditures [a]	434	100.0	585	100.0	774	100.0	749	100.0	699	100.0
Party	4	0.9	5	0.9	5	0.6	4	0.5	5	0.7
Civil [a]	28	6.4	97	16.6	120	15.5	122	16.3	131	18.7
Military	210	48.4	245	41.9	312	40.3	304	40.6	321	45.9
Loan and indemnity service	160	36.9	200	34.2	290	37.5	270	36.0	210	30.0
Other [d]	32[e]	7.4	38	6.5	47	6.1	49	6.5	32	4.6

	1933-1934		1934-1935		1935-1936		1936-1937	
	Ch$	%	Ch$	%	Ch$	%	Ch$	%
Receipts [a]	836	100.0	941	100.0	1072	100.0	1168	100.0
Revenue [a]	689	82.4	745	79.2	817	76.2	870	74.5
Customs duty	352	42.1	353	37.5	272	25.4	379	32.4
Salt tax	177	21.2	167	17.7	184	17.2	197	16.9
Commodity taxes	118	14.1	116	12.3	150	14.0	173	14.8
Other [b]	42	5.0	109[f]	11.6	211[fg]	19.7	121	10.4
Deficit covered by borrowing	147	17.6	196	20.8	255	23.8	298	25.5

Expenditures[a]	836	100.0	941	100.0	1072	100.0	1165	100.0
Party	6	0.7	6	0.6	8	0.7	—	0.6
Civil[a]	160	13.1	151	16.1	163	15.2	160	13.7
Military	373	44.6	388	41.2	390	36.4	521	44.6
Loan and indemnity service	244	29.2	238	25.3	294	27.4	302	25.9
Other	53[h]	6.3	158[eh]	16.8	217[h]	20.2	173[h]	15.2

Sources: Annual Reports of the Minister of Finance, in P. T. Chen, "Public Finance," The Chinese Year Book, 1935-1936 (Shanghai: Commercial Press, 1935), pp. 1192-1237; The Chinese Year Book, 1936-1937 (Shanghai: Commercial Press, 1936), pp. 587-588; Arthur N. Young, China's Nation-Building Effort, 1927-1937: The Financial and Economic Record (Stanford: Hoover Institution Press, 1971), pp. 433-440.

[a] Includes cost of revenue collection, except 1928-1929; excludes cash balances.

[b] Stamp tax, provincial remittances, profits of government enterprises, miscellaneous.

[c] Ch$ 62.4 million is the national revenue collected by provinces and directly disbursed for military expenses.

[d] Largely transfers to provinces from salt revenue.

[e] Capital of Central Bank, Ch$ 20 million, 1928-1929; Ch$ 74 million, 1934-1935.

[f] Government enterprises receipts, 1934-1935, Ch$ 61 million; 1935-1936, Ch$ 67 million mainly from railroads, including value of transport services for military.

[g] Includes Ch$ 78 million of various internal transfers.

[h] Includes "Reconstruction," 1933-1934, Ch$ 7 million; 1934-1935, Ch$ 26 million; 1935-1936, Ch$ 88 million; 1936-1937, Ch$ 54 million; in part this may have been investment in military-related industry.

percent of total receipts/expenditures in the still unsettled 1928-1929
fiscal year. During the next eight years this proportion varied between
a high of 81.9 percent in 1932-1933 and a low of 56.6 percent in 1935-
1936 and averaged 71.4 percent. The balance came from various miscellaneous taxes, income from government enterprises, and, above all,
from borrowing. Only in October 1936 were the first steps taken to
introduce an income tax, but the outbreak of the war in 1937 obstructed
this program. Taxation on incomes, the inheritance tax, and the wartime excess profits tax together never brought in more than 1 or 2 percent of total government receipts. Speculative commercial and financial
transactions which brought enormous profits to a few (including government "insiders") during the war and civil war were never effectively
taxed. Kuomintang fiscal policy depended on essentially regressive
indirect taxation before the war, and while 1937-1949 receipts were de-
creasingly derived from taxation, indirect taxes continued to dominate.

Foreign borrowing did not figure very largely in the finances of
the Kuomintang government before the outbreak of the war. Several
relatively small loans were made in the 1930s, including two American
commodity loans totaling US$ 26 million and some borrowing for rail-
road construction. Postwar UNRRA and ECA aid funds (not loans, of
course) were used largely to meet China's large trade deficits, but without adequate plan or control and with little benefit to the economy. Wartime credits and Lend-Lease actually utilized between 1937 and 1945
amounted to approximately US$ 2.15 billion (from the United States,
US$ 1.854; Soviet Union, US$ 173 million; Great Britain, US$ 111 million;
and France, US$ 12 million). These were received in part in the form
of military supplies and services, and in part were dissipated during
and after the war along with accumulated government foreign-exchange
holdings (obtained largely through American wartime purchases of local
currency at an inflated exchange rate) in a vain effort to maintain the
external value of the Chinese dollar. [124] In sum, foreign credits and
aid helped the Kuomintang government survive the war but contributed
nothing to prewar or postwar economic development.

The annual deficit between revenue and expenditures shown in
table 20 was met principally by domestic borrowing, which in fact after
1931-1932 annually exceeded the amount of the deficit itself, since some
of the proceeds were held as cash balances in various accounts. Between
1927 and 1935, the Finance Ministry of the Nanking government floated
thirty-eight internal loan issues with a face value of Ch$ 1,634 million.[125]
This "general purpose" borrowing was made necessary principally by
the government's heavy military costs growing out of its political in-

ability to "break any rice bowls" by reducing the swollen central and provincial armies, the mounting expenses of the campaign against the Communist-held Soviet areas, and, after 1931, the modernization of Chiang Kai-shek's forces in the face of quickening Japanese aggression.

The troubled political and economic situation in 1931 and 1932 severely depressed the Shanghai bond market, with treasury issues secured on customs revenue falling, for example, from Ch$ 62.90 in January 1931 to Ch$ 26.60 in December. Scheduled payments on the domestic debt in January 1932 were about Ch$ 200 million a third of the revenue anticipated in the fiscal year 1931-1932--and most of the internal debt was due to be retired within five years. With further borrowing impossible and faced with the prospect of default, the banks and bondholders were reluctantly forced to accept a reorganization of the debt which reduced interest payments to a fixed 6 percent and extended amortization periods to roughly double their former length. Beginning in 1933, as the effects of the world depression reached China, the pressure of deficits grew again. As table 20 shows, the amount of borrowing rose each year from fiscal 1933 to fiscal 1935 as military expenditures increased. In February 1936 a second reorganization of the internal debt was carried out by the issue of a Consolidated Loan of Ch$ 1,460 million which replaced thirty-three older issues of varying maturities and interest rates with five issues secured on the customs revenue which paid 6 percent interest and matured in twelve, fifteen, eighteen, twenty-one, and twenty-four years. In addition, a new loan of Ch$ 340 million was floated, bringing the total of domestic bond issues through 1936 to nearly Ch$ 2 billion.

The floating of this sizeable internal debt and its treatment reveal the interesting symbiotic relationship between the Kuomintang government and the Shanghai banking community, including the four large official banks. A very large part of the bond issues was absorbed by the banks. In February 1936, for example, they held two-thirds of the total outstanding issues. With few exceptions, at least before 1932, the practice of the Nanking government was to deposit bonds with the banks as collateral for cash advances of perhaps 50 to 60 percent of face value. After the issue was publicly offered and a market price established, the banks purchased the bonds from the government for the difference between the original advances and the market price. While the issuing price of most bonds might be ninety-eight, maximum quotations on the market never exceeded eighty and at times fell to as low as thirty or forty. One informed estimate is that the cash yield to the Nanking government between 1927 and 1934 from loan issues with a face value of

Ch\$ 1. 2 billion was probably in the range of 60 to 75 percent.[126] Nominal interest rates of 8. 4 to 9. 6 percent therefore actually cost the Ministry of Finance 12 to 16 percent, and, provided that interest and amortization were duly paid, bondholders might realize a 20 to 30 percent return per annum. The burden of domestic borrowing improved somewhat after the loan reorganization of 1932. Average yields on domestic bonds ranged from 15 to 24 percent through 1932, dropped to 16. 8 percent in 1933, and to 11. 6 percent in 1936.[127] Bonds were also purchased by the banks as reserves against note issues, which grew rapidly after the currency reform of 1935. Public demand for government bonds on the Shanghai market was largely for speculation rather than investment. The reorganization of the domestic debt in 1932 and 1936, which was forced upon the government by ever-mounting loan service costs, shook the market somewhat by reducing nominal interest rates and extending amortization schedules. Until wartime inflation in effect cancelled the domestic public debt--the only really "progressive taxation" during the republican era--providing credit to the government remained highly profitable to the lenders.

Resort to this high-cost credit was linked to the fact that the principal creditors, the four government banks which dominated the modern banking system, were under the influence of individuals prominent in the government who utilized these institutions both in the political intrigues of the capital and in profiting personally in the private sector of the economy. It was widely believed in the 1930s that the Central Bank of China was the preserve of K'ung Hsiang-hsi (H. H. Kung), the Bank of Communications of the "C-C Clique," the Bank of China of Sung Tzu-wen (T. V. Soong), and the Farmers Bank of China of the highest officers of the Chinese army. Personal corruption, however, is not easy to document. In any case such corruption was probably less important in its economic consequences than the diversion of scarce capital resources--which might have been used for industrial or commercial investment--to the financing of current government military expenditures or to speculation in the bond market.

It can be said that the Chinese banking system in the twentieth century failed lamentably to carry out the function of credit creation for the development of the economy as a whole. This is, of course, first to say that modern banking in China was underdeveloped. While 128 new banks were established from 1928 to 1937, and in 1937 China had 164 modern banks with 1, 597 branches, these were overwhelmingly concentrated in the major cities of the coastal provinces (Shanghai alone had 58 head offices and 130 branch offices in 1936). Modern banking facilities were meager in the agricultural interior and never adapted themselves to the credit needs of a peasant economy. The cooperative societies which grew up in the 1920s and 1930s and which might have served as intermediaries between the banking system and the peasant farmer were in fact insignificant in number and tended to provide the bulk of their credit to richer farmers who in any case could obtain loans at relatively low rates from other sources. The "native" banks (ch'ien-chuang, etc.) which survived and sometimes thrived into the 1930s tended to limit themselves to financing local trade. While the foreign banks in the treaty ports were amply supplied with funds, including large deposits by wealthy Chinese, their principal operations were the short-term financing of foreign trade and speculation in foreign exchange.

Beyond these considerations, however, the Chinese modern banking system that did develop in the decade before the war was distorted into an instrument primarily involved in financing a government which was continuously in debt. The capital and reserves of the principal modern banks increased from Ch$ 186 million in 1928 to Ch$ 447 million in 1935. Deposits during the same period increased from Ch$ 1,123 million to Ch$ 3,779 million. Much of the increment was accounted for by the growth of the "big four" government banks. In 1928 the Central Bank of China, Bank of China, Bank of Communications, and Farmers Bank of China had capital and reserves of Ch$ 64 million or 34 percent of the national total; by 1935 the figure was Ch$ 183 million or 41 percent. Deposits of the four banks totalled Ch$ 554 million or 49 percent of the national figure in 1928; by 1935 they were Ch$ 2,106 million or 56 percent. At the end of 1935 the government held Ch$ 146 million, or four-fifths, of the capital of ten banks (including the four government banks) representing 49 percent of the total capital and 61 percent of the combined resources of all modern banks. Other leading private banks were under the control or influence of the "big four," and numerous interlocking directorates tied together the principal regional banking cliques, the government banks, native banking syndicates, and the insurance, commercial, and industrial enterprises in which they invested. The largest provincial bank, that of Kwangtung, which had 40 percent of the total resources of all provincial and municipal banks, was closely linked with the Bank of China. Collaboration between the government and private banks facilitated meeting the needs of the Ministry of Finance for borrowed funds, but also diverted capital from private production and trade. Moreover, the Central Bank of China, created in 1928, did not become a true central bank with respect to the supply of money and credit; it was primarily a vehicle for the short-term financing of the government debt. [128]

In sum, this system was a centralized banking structure dominated by the four government banks, and the concentration of banking resources which it represented was in line with the general goal of "economic control" which characterized the economic thinking of the Kuomintang government. The purposes to which this control was directed, however, were not primarily economic reform and development. Credit made available by the banks to the government in the 1930s was devoted to financing the unification of China by force--the overriding priority in the eyes of the Nanking regime. Little was left for developmental expenditure despite the plan-making that kept numerous central and provincial government offices busy.

Even according to the published data for 1928-1937, which may not reveal the full amount of government military allocations, from 40 to 48 percent of annual expenditures were devoted to military purposes. Military appropriations together with loan and indemnity service--most of the borrowing was for army needs--annually accounted for 67 to 85 percent of total outlays. An unduly large part of "civil" expenditures represented the costs of tax collection--Ch\$ 60 million out of Ch\$ 120 million in 1930-1931 and Ch\$ 66 million out of Ch\$ 122 million in 1931-1932, for example. Appropriations for public works were small and welfare expenditures almost nonexistent.

While total government spending was a relatively small part of national income, the pattern of income and expenditure described above tended to have a negative effect on both economic development and the stability of the Kuomintang government. It is of course true that military outlays in the 1930s probably never exceeded 2 percent of China's gross domestic product--the 1933 ratio was 1.2 percent of GDP--and the looming Japanese threat was a real one. Furthermore, military expenditures may have substantial economic side effects: roads being built, peasant soldiers learning how to operate and repair simple machines, some industrial development (e.g., chemicals for munitions), and so on. To write "hypertrophic military establishment" (page 76) may therefore in part reflect the bad press that the Nationalist government fully earned on other counts. However, if one thinks in terms of effectively available rather than potential financial resources, it remains the case that Nanking's large military expenditures withdrew from the economy resources that alternatively could have been used for investment or consumption in the private sector of the economy without conclusively providing either an end to internal disorder or protection against Japanese encroachment. Service of the domestic debt, given the prevalence of regressive indirect taxes, tended to transfer real purchasing power from lower income groups to a small number of wealthy speculators. Since the proceeds of the loans were spent largely for military purposes and debt service, and the bondholding classes preferred speculation to productive investment, domestic borrowing produced neither public nor private expenditure aimed at increasing the output of goods such as to offset the burden on the Chinese population of the regressive national tax structure. In addition, for the private industrial entrepreneur credit was always short. A situation in which the banks in the 1930s paid 8 to 9 percent on fixed deposits which were used to purchase government bonds necessitated an interest rate on bank loans too high to permit extensive financing of private industry, commerce, and agriculture.

In the last two years before the war a mild inflationary trend had already appeared, traceable in part to the ease with which the supply of money could be expanded following the currency reform of 1935. This situation was as nothing, however, compared with the inflation which began with the outbreak of hostilities in 1937 and ended in the complete collapse of the monetary system and of the Kuomintang government in 1948-1949. China's runaway inflation was due principally to the continued fiscal deficit which was financed by ever-growing note issues. That ultimately it was caused by the Japanese seizure of China's richest provinces in the first year of the war and that it fed on eight years of war and three of civil war is undeniable, but it is equally of consequence that in the face of peril the Kuomintang government did little that was significant to stem the inflation, and the years 1937-1949 saw a remarkable continuity of economic policies which had already been defective before 1937. [129]

Table 21 shows the growth of note issue and the soaring index of prices from 1937 to 1948. Until 1940, the inflation was still moderate and for the most part confined to the more sensitive urban sector of the economy. However, the poor harvest of that year, the continued decline of food production through 1941, and the outbreak of the general Pacific war unleashed new inflationary pressures. From 1940 to 1946 annual price increases in unoccupied China averaged more than 300 percent. Prices broke briefly after the Japanese surrender in the autumn of 1945, but from November to December 1945 the price index began to climb at an unprecedented rate. There was a momentary halt in August 1948, when new Gold Yuan notes were issued, and then onward to catastrophe.

Real government revenue and expenditure both decreased drastically during the war, the former considerably more than the latter,

TABLE 21

NOTE ISSUE AND PRICE INDEX, 1937-1948

Year [a]	Note Issue Outstanding [b] (Million Chinese $)	Price Index [c] (January-June 1937 = 100)
1937	2,060	100
1938	2,740	176
1939	4,770	323
1940	8,440	724
1941	15,810	1,980
1942	35,100	6,620
1943	75,400	22,800
1944	189,500	75,500
1945	1,031,900	249,100
1946	3,726,100	627,210
1947	33,188,500	10,340,000
1948	374,762,200	287,700,000

[a] At the end of each calendar year, except 1948 where the data are for June and July respectively.

[b] 1937-1944: Arthur N. Young, China and the Helping Hand (Cambridge: Harvard University Press, 1963, pp. 435-436.

1946-1948: Chang Kia-ngau, The Inflationary Spiral: The Experience of China, 1939-1950 (New York: Wiley, 1958), p. 374.

[c] At the end of each year, except 1937 (January-June average) and 1948 (July). 1937-1945: Index of average retail prices in main cities of unoccupied China (Young, pp. 435-436); 1946-1947: all China; 1948: Shanghai (Chang, pp. 372-373.

however. The largest single source of prewar revenue, the customs
duty, was lost to the Chinese government as the Japanese quickly occupied China's coastal provinces. As the size of the territory under Kuomintang control contracted, receipts from commodity taxes and other
revenues naturally fell too. On the expenditure side, the real cost of
servicing the domestic debt was reduced radically by the inflation, while
by early 1939 payments on foreign loans secured on the customs and
salt revenue were suspended. Military expenditure, as before 1937,
dominated government outlays. Especially from 1940 on, a massive
expansion of the army occurred as Chiang Kai-shek prepared both for
a protracted resistance against Japan and a postwar showdown with the
Communists. At the end of the war the Nationalist army was five million men strong, had consumed 70 to 80 percent of government wartime
expenditures, was inadequately equipped and poorly officered, and by
its excessive recruitment of rural labor had probably contributed to a
decline of agricultural production while by its concentration near the
larger towns of unoccupied China it added enormously to the inflationary
pressure. There is little to suggest, any more than before the war,
that the size and cost of the military establishment contributed propor-
tionately to either the defense of China or the stability of the Kuomintang
government. As the civil war grew in ferocity in 1947 and 1948, the
demands of the military, supported by the leaders of the government,
shattered all checks to runaway expenditure.

Again, following a prewar pattern, insofar as the wartime Kuomintang government was financed by tax revenues, these were predominantly regressive indirect taxes. (One exception was the wartime land
tax in kind discussed above; this tax, however, hit the poor farmer
more heavily than it did the rich.) In particular, no effort was made to
tax the windfall gains of entrepreneurs and speculators who profited
immensely by the inflation. The interlude, however brief, between war
and civil war in 1945-1946, as the government returned to formerly
Japanese-occupied China, presented an opportunity to institute sweeping
and equitable tax reforms to offset the expansion of the money supply,
but it was not taken.

Wartime and postwar government expenditures, however, were
financed not by taxation but primarily by bank advances which generated
continuous increases in the note issue. The sale of bonds, even with
compulsory allocation, amounted to only 5 percent of the cumulative
deficit for the years 1937-1945 and even less during 1946-1948. After
the exclusive right to note issue was given to the Central Bank of China
in 1942, even the formality of depositing bonds with the banks as collateral for advances was dropped. Efforts to offset the inflationary effects

of the note issue and to maintain the international value of the Chinese dollar by the sale of foreign exchange or gold and the postwar importation of commodities served only to drain the country of accumulated foreign assets which might have been devoted to economic development after the defeat of Japan.

The inflation, of course, resulted from excessive monetary demand generated by the government deficit in circumstances of inadequate supply. To a limited extent the output of industrial consumer commodities in unoccupied China increased during the war, but the absolute magnitude was inconsequential in relieving the inflationary pressure. These commodities tended to be produced by small-scale private firms. In contrast, investments in producer goods industries were mainly by government or semi-official organs. In general, as in prewar China, there was no effective policy channeling scarce resources to the most essential needs. In any case, the small industrial base which was developed in the interior in wartime was virtually abandoned as the government returned to coastal China.

Whatever hopes were held that the recovery of the industrially more developed provinces of China would solve the supply problem were rudely shattered by the following circumstances: Soviet removal of major industrial equipment from Manchuria; Communist control of important parts of the north China countryside which, for example, denied raw cotton supplies to the Shanghai mills; the incompetence and corruption of the carpetbag National Resources Commission and China Textile Development Corporation which took over the operation of former Japanese and puppet firms; the absence of a rational and equitable plan to allocate the foreign exchange resources available at the war's end; and the same inability as in the pre-1937 period on the part of the Kuomintang government to control speculation, reform the tax structure, and give sufficient priority to developmental economic investment.

IX. Foreign Trade and Investment

Foreign trade and investment played a relatively small role in the Chinese economy--even in the twentieth century. The effects of the Western and Japanese economic impact must be taken into account in a consideration of various distinct sectors, but most of the Chinese economy remained beyond the reach of the foreigner.

According to estimates by C. F. Remer and the Japanese East Asia Research Institute (Tōa Kenkyūjo), foreign investment in China had reached a total of US$3,483 million by 1936, growing from US$733 million in 1902, US$1,610 million in 1914, and US$3,243 million in 1931 (table 22). On a per capita basis--taking the Chinese population in 1914 as 430 million and in 1936 as 500 million--the figures for these two years are approximately US$3.75 and US$6.97 respectively. These per capita amounts are notably smaller than foreign investment in other underdeveloped countries: for example, in 1938, India, US$20; Latin America, US$86; and Africa, excluding the Union of South Africa, US$20. Per capita foreign investment as of a given year may not be the most significant measure of the importance of that investment. Available data do not, however, permit any precise estimate of annual capital inflow figures which might be compared with national income and domestic capital formation. Very roughly, net private foreign investment in the early 1930s accounted for slightly less than 1 percent of China's GNP and about 20 percent of total investment.[130] That is, the aggregate was small but not insignificant.

Remer's data indicate that, when the annual inflow of new investment capital is balanced against outpayments of interest and amortization on government loans and profits on foreign business investments, there was a substantial net outflow of capital in these accounts in the years 1902-1931.[131] As table 27 (page 103) indicates, however, overseas Chinese remittances more than balanced this outflow, so that overall there was an inflow of capital which, together with outpayments of specie, financed China's continued excess of imports over exports. The growth in the total value of foreign investment in these circumstances, apart from the effect of the upward movement of prices, seems to have been due to reinvestment of their profits by foreigners in China. Indeed, some of the "foreign" remittances never left China, but were paid directly to foreign creditors in Shanghai or Hong Kong who plowed a substantial portion back into enterprises located in the several treaty ports. The growth of Jardine, Matheson and Company over the course of a century from a small agency house in the 1830s to the largest trading company in China with many industrial and financial interests illustrates this process quite well.

The largest foreign interest until 1931, when the Japanese seized Manchuria and began to invest heavily in its development, was that of Great Britain as table 23 shows. Of British direct investment, which accounted for 66 percent and 81 percent respectively of total British investments in 1914 and 1931, about half in 1931 was in fields directly associated with foreign trade, 21 percent in real estate, 18 percent in manufacturing, 5 percent in public utilities, 2 percent in mining, and 3 percent miscellaneous. Japanese capital in China increased rapidly

TABLE 22

FOREIGN INVESTMENTS IN CHINA, 1902-1936
(US$ Millions)

Type of Investment	1902		1914		1931		1936	
Direct investments	503.2	64%	1,067.0	66%	2,493.2	77%	2,681.7	77%
Obligations of Chinese government	284.7	36	525.8	33	710.6	22	766.7	22
Loans to private parties	0.0		17.5	1	38.7	1	34.8	1
Total	787.9	100%	1,610.3	100%	3,242.5	100%	3,483.2	100%

Source: Chi-ming Hou, Foreign Investment and Economic Development in China, 1840-1937 (Cambridge: Harvard University Press, 1965), p. 13, which in turn is based on C. F. Remer, Foreign Investments in China (New York: Macmillan, 1933) and Tōa Kenkyūjo, Rekkoku tai-Shi tōshi to Shina kokusai shūshi [Foreign investments in China and China's balance of payments] (Tokyo, 1941).

TABLE 23

FOREIGN INVESTMENT IN CHINA, 1902-1936, BY CREDITOR COUNTRY
(US$ Millions)

Country	1902		1914		1931		1936	
Great Britain	260.3	33.0%	607.5	37.7%	1,189.2	36.7%	1,220.8	35.0%
Japan	1.0	0.1	219.6	13.6	1,136.9	35.1	1,394.0	40.0
Russia	246.5	31.3	269.3	16.7	273.2	8.4	0.0	0.0
United States	19.7	2.5	49.3	3.1	196.8	6.1	298.8	8.6
France	91.1	11.6	171.4	10.7	192.4	5.9	234.1	6.7
Germany	164.3	20.9	263.6	16.4	87.0	2.7	148.5	4.3
Belgium	4.4	0.6	22.9	1.4	89.0	2.7	58.4	1.7
Netherlands	0.0		0.0		28.7	0.9	0.0	0.0
Italy	0.0		0.0		46.4	1.4	72.3	2.1
Scandinavian countries	0.0		0.0		2.9	0.1	0.0	
Others	0.6	0.1	6.7	0.4	0.0		56.3	1.6
Total	787.9	100.0%	1,610.3	100.0%	3,242.5	100.0%	3,483.2	100.0%

Source: Hou, Foreign Investment and Economic Development in China, 1840-1937, p. 17.

after 1905 when Japan became firmly entrenched in south Manchuria. Japanese direct investments, 77 percent of total foreign investments in 1931, were mainly in transportation (the South Manchurian Railway), import and export trade, manufacturing (chiefly cotton textiles), and mining. Russia's investment is accounted for almost entirely by the Chinese Eastern Railway which was sold to Japan in 1935. [132]

Direct business investment formed 66 percent, 77 percent, and 77 percent of total foreign investments in the years 1914, 1931, and 1936 respectively. The balance represented principally the borrowing of the Chinese government. C. M. Hou's recalculation of Remer's data and those of the East Asia Research Institute (table 24) indicates that in 1931 this direct investment was distributed as follows: import and export trade, 19.4 percent; railroads, 16.0 percent; manufacturing, 14.9 percent; real estate, 13.6 percent; banking and finance, 8.6 percent; shipping, 7.8 percent; mining, 4.4 percent; communications and public utilities, 4.0 percent; and miscellaneous, 11.3 percent. It is immediately evident from these figures that, in contrast to the typical pattern of foreign investment in many underdeveloped countries, very little foreign capital in China had gone into export-oriented industries such as mining or plantation agriculture. Even in Manchuria, Japanese investment in agriculture was negligible.

In those countries--much of Latin America, for example, or Indonesia under the Dutch--where foreign capital was in fact concentrated in export industries, the result had been lopsided development of the recipient economies which had come to specialize in one or more agricultural or mineral exports the market for which was extremely sensitive to foreign business cycles. Foreign investment on this pattern, moreover, had allegedly reinforced the position of the native landowning class who were the chief gainers from the commercialization of agriculture. Their increased income, however, was not invested in industrial development but was utilized in much the same way as in the past: in hoarding at home (land concentration, treaty port real estate) and now also more safely abroad (in foreign banks and securities), and in luxury consumption (import surplus). The growth of export industries also had the further consequence of attracting native capital into intermediary tertiary activities, such as petty trade ancillary to the business of foreign firms, and as a consequence is alleged to have drawn off talent and the capital that might have been employed more productively. In very limited areas, as on the southeastern coast and around Canton, some such process as the above may be discerned in China on a small scale. However, the Chinese economy in the republican era was not importantly

TABLE 24

FOREIGN DIRECT INVESTMENTS IN CHINA BY INDUSTRY
(US$ Millions)

	1914		1931		1936	
Import-export trade	142.6	13.4%	483.7	19.4%	450.2	16.8%
Banking and finance	6.3	0.6	214.7	8.6	548.7	20.5
Transportation (railroads and shipping)	336.3	31.5	592.4	23.8	669.5	25.0
Manufacturing	110.6	10.4	372.4	14.9	526.6	19.6
Mining	34.1	3.2	108.9	4.4	41.9	1.6
Communications and public utilities	23.4	2.2	99.0	4.0	138.4	5.1
Real estate	105.5	9.9	339.2	13.6	241.1	9.0
Miscellaneous	308.2	28.9	282.9	11.3	65.3	2.4
Total	1,067.0	100.0%	2,493.2	100.0%	2,681.7	100.0%

Source: Hou, Foreign Investment and Economic Development in China, 1840–1937, p. 16.

restructured by foreign capital so as to tie its fate to the vagaries of the world market.

Direct investment was heavily concentrated in the treaty ports, Shanghai in particular, until 1931 as table 25 indicates. Japanese efforts to develop a Manchurian industrial base in the 1930s were discussed above, and the share of foreign-owned factories in the manufacturing sector which was located mainly in the treaty ports was suggested in tables 9 and 10 (pages 35 and 37). To many commentators, foreign-owned enterprises and foreign investment (which is often equated with control) in Chinese enterprises were primarily responsible for obstructing the development of Chinese modern industry. Chinese firms simply could not compete successfully with foreign firms which had larger revenues, better technology and management, enjoyed the privileges of extra-territoriality and exemption from Chinese taxes, and were free from the depredations of Chinese officialdom. To counter this "oppression argument" C. M. Hou has shown that, far from being overwhelmed, Chinese-owned modern enterprises maintained a "remarkably stable" share of the modern sector over the years before 1937. [133] Although it might be argued that in the absence of foreign competition Chinese firms might have grown even faster, it is by no means certain that without the "exogenous shock" of foreign trade and investment the premodern economy of nineteenth-century China would have been capable of embarking at all on the path of development. [134]

TABLE 25

GEOGRAPHICAL DISTRIBUTION OF FOREIGN INVESTMENTS
IN CHINA, 1902, 1914, 1931
(US$ Millions)

	1902		1914		1931	
Shanghai	110.0	14.0%	291.0	18.1%	1,112.2	34.3%
Manchuria	216.0	27.4	361.6	22.4	880.0	27.1
Rest of China	177.2	22.5	433.1	26.9	607.8	18.8
Undistributed	284.7	36.1	524.6	32.6	642.5	19.8
Total	787.9	100.0%	1,610.3	100.0%	3,242.5	100.0%

Source: Remer, Foreign Investments in China, p. 73.

Apart from railroad construction and industrial loans, it is doubtful that Chinese government borrowing abroad was of any advantage to the Chinese economy. The relatively high service costs of these obligations (interest, discounts, commissions) were excessive considering the small benefit derived from them. An analysis of the indebtedness incurred during the period 1912-1937 according to the purposes for which the borrowed funds were utilized seems to support the conclusion that foreign borrowing tended to be economically sterile.[135] Approximately 8.5 percent (in constant 1913 prices) of the total was borrowed for military purposes and indemnity payments to foreigners. Another 43.3 percent was earmarked for general administrative purposes, which meant largely for interest payments on the foreign debt itself. While the 36.9 percent accounted for by railroad loans was a potentially productive investment, its usefulness was limited by endemic civil wars and disturbances, and by provisions in the loan agreements which prevented efficient central management by establishing boundaries within which the several lines were treated as separate enterprises. Telephone and telegraph loans constituted the largest part of the 10.8 percent accounted for by industrial loans.

In view of the paucity of useful national income data, the ratio of total foreign trade turnover to national product during the republican era can only be roughly estimated. In 1933, the one year for which an acceptable measure of domestic product is available, imports and exports together were valued at 7 percent of gross domestic product. This was, however, after the loss of Manchuria whose foreign trade was not insubstantial and after the onset of the great depression. In the late 1920s China's foreign trade was probably equal to somewhat more than 10 percent of national product. This is a relatively low proportion but not abnormally low in terms of international comparisons given China's size, level of development, distance from major maritime routes, abundant resources, and large domestic market. Values and index number of China's foreign trade for the years 1912-1936 are given in table 26.

In current prices there was a slow growth of both imports and exports from the 1880s to 1900. Growth was more rapid from 1901 to 1918, and then noticeably accelerated from 1919 to 1931. Measured in terms of quantity rather than value, trade grew somewhat less rapidly. Imports were fairly steady in the last two decades of the nineteenth century; from 1900 there was a steady upward trend broken only by the disruptions resulting from World War I which, we have noted, allowed some leeway for the growth of Chinese industry. Exports grew steadily from about 1907. Available data indicate that the trend in the simple terms

TABLE 26

VALUES AND INDEX NUMBERS OF FOREIGN TRADE, 1912–1936

Year	Value in Current Prices [a]			Index of Value of Total Trade (1913 = 100)	Indices of Quantity (1913 = 100)		Terms of Trade (Import Price/ Export Price) (1913 = 100)
	Net Imports	Net Exports	Import Surplus		Imports	Exports	
1912	473	371	102	86.7	82.8	103.8	112.9
1913	570	403	167	100.0	100.0	100.0	100.0
1914	569	356	213	95.1	91.6	83.8	103.3
1915	454	419	35	89.7	70.3	96.5	104.8
1916	516	482	34	102.5	73.7	102.3	104.6
1917	550	463	87	104.0	73.4	108.3	123.4
1918	555	486	69	106.9	66.1	105.5	128.4
1919	647	631	16	131.3	75.4	140.0	134.1
1920	762	542	220	133.9	75.9	119.3	155.6
1921	906	601	305	154.8	94.7	126.9	142.3
1922	945	655	290	164.4	112.6	130.5	117.7
1923	923	753	170	172.2	108.5	137.3	109.1
1924	1,018	772	246	183.9	119.6	136.6	105.4

Year							
1925	948	776	172	177.1	109.9	132.9	103.5
1926	1,124	864	260	204.2	130.5	141.1	98.6
1927	1,013	919	94	198.4	109.8	154.1	108.6
1928	1,196	991	205	224.6	131.5	156.1	100.4
1929	1,266	1,016	250	234.4	139.9	149.2	93.1
1930	1,310	895	115	226.5	131.0	131.1	102.5
1931	1,433	909	524	240.7	129.9	136.5	116.0
1932	1,049	493	556	158.4	106.0	100.8	128.6
1933	864 (1,346)	393 (612)	471 (734)	129.1	97.5	124.?	142.7
1934	661 (1,030)	344 (536)	317 (494)	103.2	85.1	115.3	136.1
1935	590 (919)	370 (576)	220 (343)	98.6	83.6	123.7	122.9
1936	604 (942)	453 (707)	151 (235)	108.6	77.9	125.6	109.4

Sources: Hsiao Liang-lin, China's Foreign Trade Statistics, 1864–1949 (Cambridge: Harvard University Press, 1974), pp. 23–24, 274–275; Yu-kwei Cheng, Foreign Trade and Industrial Development of China (Washington: The University Press of Washington, D. C., 1956 , p. 259.

ᵃ In millions Haikwan taels; from 1933 trade was valued in Ch$ as shown in parentheses.

of trade--it is not easy to calculate the more significant single factoral
terms of trade which take account of changes in productivity of exports--
was against China (see table 26), but this trend would only be significant
to the degree that the Chinese economy was linked to the world market
as a result of expanding foreign trade. In the case of China that linkage
was of less importance than in many other underdeveloped countries.

In all the years of the republic, as had been the case since the
1880s, China's foreign trade was marked by an import surplus, and the
current account balance was consistently unfavorable. China's ability
to sustain merchandise imports in excess of merchandise exports to a
large extent appears to have been due to remittances from overseas Chinese, which year after year flowed back to the homeland, as well as to
new foreign investment. All available estimates of China's balance of
international payments, however, include a substantial amount "un-
accounted for" even after remittances and investment are considered.
The estimates in table 27 for 1903, 1930, and 1935 are by H. B. Morse,
C. F. Remer, and the Bank of China respectively.

In the mid-nineteenth century China's principal exports had been
silk and tea. They accounted for 92 percent of the total in 1871, dropped
to about 80 percent during the 1880s, to approximately 50 percent in 1898,
and continued to decline thereafter as table 28 indicates. While they
continued to be predominantly natural resource products, China's exports
were considerably diversified in the course of the twentieth century.
The principal new export was the soybean and its products, grown largely
in Manchuria. Of growing importance, too, were the exports of iron
ore and coal to Japan, and the shipment of cotton yarn to Japan by Japanese-owned spinning mills in China.

Until the 1890s when it was surpassed by cotton cloth and yarn,
opium was the most important import into China. About 1900, cotton
cloth and yarn constituted 40 percent of total imports. The growth of
Chinese- and foreign-owned textile mills in China led to a decline in
cotton textile imports. To supply these new mills, however, China became a significant importer of raw cotton. By 1936, domestic cotton
output was almost able to meet the demand; but in the post-1945 period
raw cotton was again critically short, testifying both to the decline of
agricultural production and to the disruption of transport by the civil
war. In general, the proportion of industrial raw materials and equipment in total imports grew steadily but very slowly, while such manufactured consumer goods as textiles, cigarettes, and matches declined.
In the late 1920s and early 1930s, rice, wheat, and wheat flour climbed
in importance among imports but then fell again with economic recovery

TABLE 27

BALANCE OF INTERNATIONAL PAYMENTS
(Millions Chinese $)

	1903	1930	1935
Current outpayments:			
Merchandise imports	492	1, 965	1, 129
Specie imports	58	101	---
Service of foreign loans	69	111	108
Chinese expenditures abroad	7	13	55
Remittances of foreign enterprises and other profits	35	227	55
Total	661	2, 417	1, 347
Current inpayments:			
Merchandise exports	374	1, 476	662
Specie exports	51	48	357
Foreign expenditures in China	81	218	150
Overseas remittances	114	316	260
Total	620	2, 058	1, 429
Capital inpayments:			
New foreign investments in China	42	202	140
Unaccounted for:	(−1)	(−157)	222

Source: Li Choh-ming, "International Trade," in China, ed.
    H. F. MacNair (Berkeley: University of California Press,
    1946), p. 501.

in 1935 and 1936. Rural and especially urban population growth, lagging
agricultural output, and poor transportation made the task of feeding
China's urban population always a difficult one.

Table 29 shows the proportion of China's trade with her leading
suppliers and customers. There was a gradual diversification of trade
between 1906 and 1936 as the growing percentage attributable to "others"
indicates. (The apparent sharp drop in imports from Hong Kong is the
result of a new invoice system, introduced in 1932, intended to identify
the actual national origin of goods shipped to China through Hong Kong.)
Great Britain, Japan, and the United States were China's principal
trading partners. Japanese trade was predominant in Manchuria and
north China and smallest in the south. The reverse was true of Britain.

TABLE 28

COMPOSITION OF FOREIGN TRADE
(Percentage of Current Value)

	1913	1916	1920	1925	1928	1931	1936
Imports:							
Cotton goods	19.3	14.1	21.8	16.3	14.2	7.6	1.5
Cotton yarn	12.7	12.4	10.6	4.4	1.6	0.3	0.2
Raw cotton	0.5	1.6	2.4	7.4	5.7	12.6	3.8
Rice and wheat	3.3	6.6	0.8	6.8	5.7	10.6	4.1
Wheat flour	1.8	0.2	0.3	1.6	2.6	2.0	0.5
Sugar	6.4	7.1	5.2	9.5	8.3	6.0	2.2
Tobacco	2.9	5.8	4.7	4.1	5.1	4.4	1.8
Paper	1.3	1.8	1.9	2.0	2.4	3.2	4.1
Kerosene	4.5	6.2	7.1	7.0	5.2	4.5	4.2
Petroleum	--	0.2	0.4	0.9	1.4	1.8	4.1
Transportation materials	0.8	4.0	2.6	1.9	2.3	2.3	5.6
Chemicals, dyes, and pigments	5.6	4.1	6.4	5.6	7.5	8.0	10.8
Iron, steel, and other metals	5.3	5.1	8.3	4.7	5.4	6.2	13.2

Machinery	1.4	1.3	3.2	1.8	1.8	3.1	6.4
All others	34.2	29.5	24.3	26.0	30.8	27.4	37.5
Total	100.0	100.0	100.0	100.0	100.0	100.0	100.0
Exports:							
Silk and silk goods	25.3	22.3	18.6	22.5	18.4	13.3	7.8
Tea	8.4	9.0	1.6	2.9	5.7	3.6	4.3
Beans and bean cake	12.0	9.3	13.0	15.9	20.5	21.4	1.3
Seeds and oil	7.8	8.4	9.1	7.9	8.3	8.4	18.7
Eggs and egg products	1.4	2.6	4.0	4.3	4.4	4.1	5.9
Hides, leather, and skins	6.0	6.0	4.3	4.0	5.4	4.1	5.7
Ores and metals	3.3	6.3	3.2	2.9	2.1	1.6	7.7
Coal	1.6	1.2	2.3	2.6	2.9	3.0	1.6
Cotton yarn and cotton goods	0.6	0.8	1.4	2.0	3.3	4.9	3.0
Raw cotton	4.0	3.6	1.7	3.8	3.1	2.9	4.0
All others	29.6	30.5	40.8	31.2	29.5	32.7	40.0
Total	100.0	100.0	100.0	100.0	100.0	100.0	100.0

Source: Yu-kwei Cheng, Foreign Trade and Industrial Development of China, pp. 32, 34.

TABLE 29

DISTRIBUTION OF FOREIGN TRADE AMONG TRADING PARTNERS
(Percentage of Current Value)

	1906	1913	1919	1927	1931	1936
Imports from:						
Great Britain	18.4	16.5	9.5	7.3	8.3	11.7
Hong Kong	33.8	29.3	22.6	20.6	15.3	1.9
Japan and Taiwan	14.3	20.4	36.3	28.4	20.0	16.3
U.S.A.	10.4	6.0	16.2	16.1	22.2	19.6
Russia	0.1	3.8	2.1	2.2	1.7	0.1
France	1.0	0.9	0.5	1.4	1.5	2.0
Germany	4.0	4.8	---	3.8	5.8	15.9
Others	18.0	18.3	12.8	20.2	25.2	32.5
Total	100.0	100.0	100.0	100.0	100.0	100.0
Exports to:						
Great Britain	5.6	4.1	9.1	6.3	7.1	9.2
Hong Kong	35.0	29.0	20.8	18.5	16.3	15.1
Japan and Taiwan	14.1	16.2	30.9	22.7	27.4	14.5
U.S.A.	10.9	9.3	16.0	13.3	13.2	26.4
Russia	7.9	11.1	3.4	8.4	6.0	0.6
France	10.7	10.1	5.4	5.6	3.8	4.3
Germany	2.4	4.2	---	2.2	2.5	5.5
Others	13.4	16.0	14.4	23.0	23.7	24.4
Total	100.0	100.0	100.0	100.0	100.0	100.0

Source: Yu-kwei Cheng, Foreign Trade and Industrial Development of China, pp. 20, 48-49.

American trade, which exceeded that of all other countries in the mid-1930s, was concentrated in central China. The decline in Japan's share after 1931 is to some degree a measure of the effectiveness of Chinese boycotts following the "Mukden incident."

The question remains of the overall consequences for China's economy of the patterns of foreign trade and investment just described. I have been categorical in stating that in aggregate terms they bulked much smaller than in many other underdeveloped economies. Yet to many Chinese and foreign observers these were the most critical influences shaping the course of modern Chinese history. The difficulty here, I suggest, is one of precipitating out purely economic factors from the complex mixture that was the foreign impact upon twentieth-century China.[136] China was changed by her modern encounter with the West, and it was the hope of economic gain which first brought the foreigner and his ways to the Middle Kingdom. Foreign economic activity was largely responsible for calling forth a small modern sector of Chinese- and foreign-owned trading and manufacturing enterprises on the fringe of the Chinese empire. The Chinese economy as a whole, however, underwent no significant transformation; at best there occurred only a "partial development." The large foreign role in the modern sector of the economy--based on an artificially low tariff and the privileges of extraterritoriality, supported by highly developed industrial economies at home, and abetted by the siphoning off of capital in indemnity and loan payments to foreign creditors--cannot be made to bear more than a part of the obloquy for this stagnation. To do more than this is to obscure the ideological and political disequilibrium which was the most profound consequence of the impact of the West and which for decades obstructed the emergence of a new political integration capable of replacing the Confucian imperial pattern of the past and taking advantage of the possibilities of economic development inherent in modern industrial technology.

The Chinese economy, in the years covered by this monograph at least, did not occupy center stage in the unfolding of the drama of Chinese history. It was only a bit player--with a few choice lines perhaps--waiting on the words of emperors, bureaucrats, diplomats, generals, propagandists, and party organizers.

NOTES

1. This monograph excludes any consideration of Communist controlled China which included areas inhabited by some ninety million persons in 1945 and operated in part with different economic assumptions. See Peter Schran, Guerilla Economy: The Development of the Shensi-Kansu-Ninghsia Border Region, 1937-1945 (Albany: University of New York Press, 1976).

2. G. William Skinner, "Marketing and Social Structure in Rural China," Part I, The Journal of Asian Studies, 26.1 (November 1964):3-44; Parts II and III in subsequent issues.

3. The characterization is Mark Elvin's, in The Chinese City between Two Worlds, ed. Mark Elvin and G. William Skinner (Stanford: Stanford University Press, 1974), p. 3.

4. These are surely very rough estimates, but they are consistent with what little hard data are available. See Gilbert Rozman, Urban Networks in Ch'ing China and Tokugawa Japan (Princeton: Princeton University Press, 1973), pp. 99-104; Dwight H. Perkins, Agricultural Development in China, 1368-1968 (Chicago: Aldine, 1969), "Urban Population Statistics (1900-1958)" (Appendix E), pp. 290-296; and H. O. Kung, "The Growth of Population in Six Large Chinese Cities," Chinese Economic Journal, 20.3 (March 1937):301-314.

5. Rhoads Murphey, The Outsiders: The Western Experience in India and China (Ann Arbor: The University of Michigan Press, 1977), provides a major reexamination of the treaty port experience.

6. Ministry of Agriculture and Commerce, Nung-shang t'ung-chi piao, 1912-1921 農商統計表 [Tables of agricultural and commercial statistics] (Shanghai, 1914-1919; Peking, 1920-1924). The volumes for 1914 and 1918 are relatively better than the others; as a whole the data are estimates rather than the products of controlled surveys.

109

7. Ministry of Communications (from 1925 issue, Ministry of Railways, Bureau of Railway Statistics), Statistics of Government Railways, 1915-1936 (from 1922 issue, Statistics of Railways) (Peking, 1916-1928; Nanking, 1931-1936).

8. The Customs statistics are usefully collated, with full references to the original sources, in Hsiao Liang-lin, China's Foreign Trade Statistics, 1864-1949 (Cambridge: Harvard University Press, 1974).

9. Ministry of Finance, Annual Reports for the 17th, 18th, 19th, 21st, 22nd, and 23rd Fiscal Years (Nanking, 1930-1936).

10. John Lossing Buck, Land Utilization in China: A Study of 16,786 Farms in 168 Localities, and 38,256 Farm Families in Twenty-Two Provinces of China, 1929-1933, 3 vols. (Nanking: University of Nanking, 1937). Volume 2 presents Buck's statistics in 475 folio pages.

11. Liu Ta-chün (D. K. Lieu) 劉大鈞 , Chung-kuo kung-yeh tiao-ch'a pao-kao 中國工業調查報告 [Report on a survey of China's industry], 3 vols. (Nanking, 1937).

12. See John Young, The Research Activities of the South Manchurian Railway Company, 1907-1945: A History and Bibliography (New York: East Asian Institute, Columbia University, 1966).

13. See Nankai Institute of Economics, 1913 nien - 1952 nien Nan-k'ai chih-su tzu-liao hui-pien 1913 年 - 1952 年南開指數資料彙編 [Nankai index numbers, 1913-1952] (Peking: T'ung-chi, 1958).

14. Published in its bilingual monthly journal, Ching-chi t'ung-chi yüeh-chih 經濟統計月誌 [The Chinese Economic and Statistical Review, 1934-1941]. Shanghai price indices are collected in Academy of Sciences, Shanghai Institute of Economic Research, Shang-hai chieh-fang ch'ien-hou wu-chia tzu-liao hui-pien, 1921 nien - 1957 nien 上海解放前後物價資料滙編 1921 年 - 1957 年 [Collected materials on Shanghai prices before and after Liberation, 1921-1957] (Shanghai: Jen-min, 1958).

15. Chang Kia-ngau, The Inflationary Spiral: The Experience of China, 1939-1950 (New York: M.I.T. Press and Wiley, 1958), includes data available only to the author who was governor of the Central Bank of China.

16. The introductory matter to each of the thirty-six sections of National Government, Directorate of Statistics, Chung-hua min-kuo t'ung-chi t'i-yao, 1935 中華民國統計提要 [Statistical abstract of the Republic of China, 1935] (Nanking, 1936), includes useful descriptions of most of the statistical publications of republican China. Yen Chung-p'ing 嚴中平 , comp., Chung-kuo chin-tai ching-chi shih t'ung-chi tzu-liao hsuan-chi 中國近代經濟史資料選輯 [Selected statistics on China's modern economic history] (Peking: K'o-hsüeh, 1955) (hereafter cited as Yen, Statistics), draws on a wide range of carefully noted sources and--in spite of its tendentious arrangement and commentaries, not to speak of the compiler's apparent innocence about "the index number problem"--is of substantial value.

17. About 470 million seems to be a charmed number for official population estimates in the 1920s and 1930s: the Nanking government Ministry of the Interior attempted a "census" in 1928, which produced an estimate of 474,787,386 based on "reports" from sixteen provinces and special municipalities and guesses by the Ministry for seventeen provinces. The same Ministry published a figure of 471,245,763 in 1938 compiled from local "reports" for 1936-1937.

18. The largest discrepancy between the Liu-Yeh and Ou estimates is in the figures for net value added by agriculture, and within agriculture for the value of crops. While Ou's figures are probably too low, Perkins has made a plausible case that those of Liu-Yeh are based on too high a grain-yield estimate for 1933. Perkins, Agricultural Development in China, pp. 29-32 and Appendix D.

19. This summary discussion follows Dwight H. Perkins, "Growth and Changing Structure of China's Twentieth-Century Economy," in China's Modern Economy in Historical Perspective, ed. Perkins (Stanford: Stanford University Press, 1975), pp. 116-125.

20. Ou Pao-san (Wu Pao-san) 巫寶三 , "Chung-kuo kuo-min so-te, 1933, 1936, chi 1946" 中國國民所得 1933, 1936, 及 1946 [China's national income of China, 1933, 1936, and 1946], She-hui k'o-hsüeh tsa-chih 社會科學雜誌, [Quarterly Review of Social Sciences], 9.2 (December 1947): 12-30, estimates national income in 1946 as 6 percent lower than 1933 (in 1933 prices). On Shanghai workers, see A. Doak Barnett, China on the Eve of Communist Takeover (New York: Praeger, 1963), pp. 78-80; on the north China rural economy during 1937-1949, Ramon H. Myers, The Chinese Peasant Economy: Agricultural Development in Hopei

and Shantung, 1890-1949 (Cambridge: Harvard University Press, 1970), pp. 278-287; on wartime unoccupied China and postwar inflation, Chang, The Inflationary Spiral, pp. 59-103.

21. Perkins, "Growth and Changing Structure of China's Twentieth-Century Economy," p. 124, who cites Myers, The Chinese Peasant Economy, pp. 234-240, and Perkins, Agricultural Development in China, chap. 5.

22. Albert Feuerwerker, "Economic Trends in the Late Ch'ing Empire, 1870-1911," in Cambridge History of China, ed. J. K. Fairbank and Denis Twitchett (Cambridge: Cambridge University Press, forthcoming).

23. Ch'en Chen 陳真 and others, comps., Chung-kuo chin-tai kung-yeh shih tzu-liao 中國近代工業史資料 [Source materials on China's modern industrial history], 4 vols. (Peking: San-lien, 1957-1961), 1:55-56 (hereafter cited as Ch'en, Industrial History).

24. Nankai Institute of Economics, Nankai Weekly Statistical Service, 4.33 (August 17, 1931):157-158.

25. See note 11 above. "Factory" was defined according to the 1929 Factory Law as an enterprise using mechanical power and employing thirty or more workers.

26. Ou Pao-san (Wu Pao-san) 巫寶三 , Chung-kuo min-kuo so-te i-chiu-san-san-nien 中國國民所得一九三三年 [China's national income, 1933], 2 vols. (Shanghai: Chung-hua, 1947), 1, tables 1-2 following p. 64 and table 5, pp. 70-71; additional data in Ou, "Chung-kuo kuo-min so-te i-chiu-san-san hsiu-cheng" 中國國民所得一九三三年修正 [Corrections to China's National Income, 1933], She-hui k'o-hsüeh tsa-chih, 9.2 (December 1947):130-136, 144-147, which incorporated the estimates of Wang Fu-san 汪馥蓀 , "Chan-ch'ien Chung-kuo kung-yeh sheng-ch'an chung wai-ch'ang sheng-ch'an ti pi-chung wen-t'i" 戰前中國工業生產中外廠生產的比重問題 [The proportion of industrial production by foreign-owned factories in total industrial production in prewar China], Chung-yang yin-hang yüeh-pao 中央銀行月報 , 2.3 (March 1947):1-19.

27. Ch'en, Industrial History, 4:92.

28. Ch'en, Industrial History, 1:89-97; 4:93-96, excerpts from Directorate of Economic Statistics, "Hou-fang kung-yeh kai-k'uang t'ung-
chi" 後方工業概況統計 [Statistics on industry in
the interior], May 1943.

29. Yen, Statistics, pp. 147-150; Wang Fu-sun 汪馥蓀, "Chan-
shih Hua-pei kung-yeh tzu-pen jiu-yeh yü sheng-ch'an" 戰時
華北工業資本就業與生產 [Wartime industrial
capital, employment, and production in north China], She-hui k'o-
hsüeh tsa-chih, 9.2 (December 1947):48.

30. Wang Chi-shen 王季深, Chan-shih Shang-hai ching-chi 戰時
上海經濟 [The economy of wartime Shanghai] (Shanghai:
Shang-hai ching-chi yen-chiu so, 1945), pp. 192, 194. I am
grateful to Professor Thomas Rawski for this reference.

31. Alexander Eckstein, Kang Chao, and John Chang, "The Economic
Development of Manchuria: The Rise of a Frontier Economy,"
The Journal of Economic History, 34.1 (March 1974):251-260.

32. Substantial data on the relative positions of state-owned and private
mining and producers' goods enterprises 1938-1948 may be found
in Ch'en, Industrial History, 3:1439-1443, 873-879, and 882-887.

33. State Statistical Bureau, Industrial Statistics Department, Wo-kuo
kang-t'ieh, tien-li, mei-t'an, chi-hsieh, fang-chih, tsao-chih kung-
yeh ti chiu-hsi 我國鋼鐵,電力,煤炭,機械,紡織,
造紙工業的今昔 [Past and present of China's iron and
steel, electric power, coal, machinery, textile, and paper indus-
tries] (Peking: T'ung-chi ch'u-pan-she, 1958), pp. 148-149; Ch'en,
Industrial History, 3:1051-1074.

34. John K. Chang, Industrial Development in Pre-Communist China:
A Quantitative Analysis (Chicago: Aldine, 1969), pp. 70-74.

35. Ou, "Chung-kuo kuo-min so-te i-chiu-san-san hsiu-cheng," pp. 137-
142, shows the net value added by handicrafts as 72 percent for all
industries, based however on a definition of "factory" which includes
only firms employing thirty or more workers and using mechanical
power.

36. This theme is implied in the arrangement of the materials in P'eng
Tse-i 彭澤益, comp., Chung-kuo chin-tai shou-kung-yeh shih

114

tzu-liao, 1840-1949 中國近代手工業史資料 ,
1840-1949 [Source materials on the history of the handicraft industry
in modern China, 1840-1949], 4 vols. (Peking: San-lien, 1957),
which otherwise provides valuable documentation that has not yet
been adequately exploited.

37. See Feuerwerker, "Economic Trends in the Late Ch'ing Empire,
     1870-1911," in Cambridge History, ed. Fairbank and Twitchett.

38. See P'eng, Chung-kuo chin-tai shou-kung-yeh shih tzu-liao, 1840-
     1949, 2:331-449.

39. See Lillian Ming-tse Li, "Kiangnan and the Silk Export Trade, 1842-
     1937," (Ph.D. dissertation, Harvard University, 1975), pp. 234-273.

40. Reynolds' results for 1875 and 1905, arrived at by a much different
     route, are very close to my estimates in "Handicraft and Manufac-
     tured Cotton Textiles in China, 1871-1910," The Journal of Economic
     History, 30.2 (June 1970):338-378. I use his figures here rather
     than my own because they are part of a methodologically consistent
     estimate for the whole period 1875-1931.

41. See Kang Chao, "The Growth of a Modern Cotton Textile Industry
     and the Competition with Handicrafts," in China's Modern Economy
     in Historical Perspective, ed. Perkins, pp. 167-201.

42. Chao (note 41), pp. 173-175, offers examples.

43. Ta-chung Liu and Kung-chia Yeh, The Economy of the Chinese
     Mainland: National Income and Economic Development, 1933-1959
     (Princeton: Princeton University Press, 1965), pp. 142-143, 512-
     513; Hsiao, China's Foreign Trade Statistics, 1864-1949, pp. 32-33.

44. Chi-ming Hou, Foreign Investment and Economic Development in
     China, 1840-1937 (Cambridge: Harvard University Press, 1965),
     pp. 169-170.

45. Li, "Kiangnan and the Silk Export Trade, 1842-1937," pp. 266-273.

46. Perkins, Agricultural Development in China, pp. 29-30.

47. Perkins, "Growth and Changing Structure of China's Twentieth-
     Century Economy," pp. 122-123.

48. Ku Ch'un-fan (Koh Tso-fan) 谷春帆 , Chung-kuo kung-yeh-hua t'ung-lun 中國工業化通論 [A general discussion of China's industrialization] (Shanghai: Commercial Press, 1947), p. 170.

49. On the origins, recruitment, wages, and working conditions of labor in the 1920s, see Jean Chesneaux, The Chinese Labor Movement, 1919-1927 (Stanford: Stanford University Press, 1968), pp. 48-112. The structure of industrial wages before 1949 is analyzed in Christopher Howe, Wage Patterns and Wage Policy in Modern China, 1919-1972 (Cambridge: Cambridge University Press, 1973), pp. 16-27. For an example of Japanese-style "permanent" employment for skilled male workers, see Andersen, Meyer and Company Limited of China (Shanghai: Kelley and Walsh, 1931), p. 114. I am indebted to Professor Thomas Rawski for this last reference.

50. Kang Chao, "Policies and Performance in Industry," in Economic Trends in Communist China, ed. Alexander Eckstein, Walter Galenson, and Ta-ching Liu (Chicago: Aldine, 1968), table 3, p. 579.

51. Feng-hwa Mah, The Foreign Trade of Mainland China (Chicago: Aldine, 1971), Appendix C, pp. 194-200.

52. Thomas G. Rawski, "The Growth of Producer Industries, 1900-1971," in China's Modern Economy in Historical Perspective, ed. Perkins, pp. 228-232.

53. Perkins, "Growth and Changing Structure of China's Twentieth-Century Economy," p. 125.

54. Perkins, Agricultural Development in China, pp. 233-240.

55. These are data for China as a whole, including Manchuria. For north China, see Myers, The Chinese Peasant Economy, pp. 177-206; many local studies are summarized in Amano Motonosuke 天野元之助 , Chūgoku nōgyō no shomondai 中國農業の諸問題 [Problems of Chinese agriculture], 2 vols. (Tokyo: Gihōdō, 1952-1953), 1:3-148.

56. For rice, wheat, and wheat flour imports, see Hsiao, China's Foreign Trade Statistics, 1864-1949, pp. 32-34; Wu Pao San 巫寶三 , Chung-kuo liang-shih tui-wai mao-i ch'i ti-wei ch'ü-shih chi pien-ch'ien chih yuan-yin, 1912-1931 中國糧食對

116

外貿易其地位趨勢及變遷之原因 [Causes
of trends and fluctuations in China's foreign trade in food grains,
1912-1931] (Nanking, 1934).

57.   Hsiao, China's Foreign Trade Statistics, 1864-1949, pp. 274-275.

58.   Amano Motonosuke 天野元之助 , Shina nōgyō keizai ron
      支那農業經濟論 [A treatise on the Chinese farm econ-
      omy], 2 vols. (Tokyo: Kaizōsha, 1940-1942), 2:696-698 (hereafter
      cited as Amano, Farm Economy), provides a listing of civil wars,
      floods, droughts, pestilence, and the provinces affected, 1912-1931.
      See also Buck, Land Utilization in China, Statistics, pp. 13-20, for
      "calamities" by locality during 1904-1929.

59.   Amano Motonosuke 天野元之助 , Chūgoku nōgyō shi kenkyū
      中國農業史研究 [A study of the history of Chinese
      agriculture] (Tokyo: Ochanomizu, 1962), pp. 389-423, for example,
      on rice technology. F. H. King, Farmers of Forty Centuries, 2nd
      ed. (London: J. Cape, 1927), provides a vivid description of the
      "permanent agriculture in China, Korea and Japan" in the early
      twentieth century.

60.   Li Wen-chih 李文治 and Chang Yu-i 章有義 , comps.,
      Chung-kuo chin-tai nung-yeh shih tzu-liao 中國近代農
      業史資料 [Source materials on China's modern agricultural
      history], 3 vols. (Peking: San-lien, 1957), 2:182 (hereafter cited
      as Chang, Agricultural History). The first volume in this collection,
      edited by Li, covers 1840-1911; the second and third, edited by
      Chang, cover 1912-1927 and 1927-1937 respectively.

61.   Ramon H. Myers, "Agrarian Policy and Agricultural Transforma-
      tion: Mainland China and Taiwan, 1895-1954," Hsiang-kang Chung-
      wen ta-hsueh Chung-kuo wen-hua yen-chiu-so hsueh-pao 香港中
      文大學中國文化研究所學報 [Journal of the Insti-
      tute of Chinese Studies of the Chinese University of Hong Kong],
      3.2 (1970): 532-535.

62.   Eckstein, Chao, Chang, "The Economic Development of Manchuria:
      The Rise of a Frontier Economy," pp. 240-251.

63.   Chang, Agricultural History, 3:476-480, 622-641.

64.   Chang, Agricultural History, 3:480-485.

65. Nung-ch'ing pao-kao 農情報告, 7.4 (April 1939):49-50, in Chang, Agricultural History, 3:708-710.

66. Perkins, Agricultural Development in China, p. 136; Chang, Agricultural History, 2:131-300; Chang Jen-chieh 張人价, Konan no beikoku 湖南 の 米穀 [Rice in Hunan], trans. of 1936 report by Hunan provincial economic research institute (Tokyo: Seikatsusha, 1940), pp. 87-113.

67. Liu and Yeh, The Economy of the Chinese Mainland, table 10 n, 68.

68. Perkins, Agricultural Development in China, pp. 35-36; Chang, Agricultural History, 2:106-407; Buck, Land Utilization in China, pp. 281-282.

69. See Myers, The Chinese Peasant Economy, passim.

70. Robert Ash, Land Tenure in Pre-Revolutionary China: Kiangsu Province in the 1920s and 1930s (London: Contemporary China Institute, School of Oriental and African Studies, 1976), p. 50. Ash himself also gives some weight to the more "purely economic factors." His study, however, appears unconvincing in its evaluation of the degree and sources of agricultural investment in twentieth-century Kiangsu.

71. Carl Riskin, "Surplus and Stagnation in Modern China," in China's Modern Economy in Historical Perspective, ed. Perkins, p. 59.

72. Riskin, "Surplus and Stagnation in Modern China," pp. 68, 74, 77-81; Victor D. Lippit, Land Reform and Economic Development in China (White Plains, N.Y.: IASP, 1974), pp. 36-94.

73. Buck, Land Utilization in China, pp. 269-270.

74. Buck, Land Utilization in China, pp. 181-185, 294, 297.

75. Buck, Land Utilization in China, pp. 193-196.

76. Perkins, Agricultural Development in China, pp. 87, 89; Lippit, Land Reform and Economic Development in China, p. 95; Kenneth R. Walker, Planning in Chinese Agriculture: Socialisation and the Private Sector, 1956-1962 (Chicago: Aldine, 1965), p. 5.

118

77. See Muramatsu Yūji 村松祐次, <u>Kindai Kōnan no sosan--</u>
<u>Chūgoku jinushi seido no kenkyū</u> 近代江南の租棧 —
中國地主制度の研究 [Bursaries in modern
Kiangnan--a study of the Chinese landlord system] (Tokyo: Tokyo
University Press, 1970), pp. 47-237, 391-636; and "A Documentary
Study of Chinese Landlordism in Late Ch'ing and Early Republican
Kiangnan," <u>Bulletin of the School of Oriental and African Studies</u>,
29.3 (1966): 566-599.

78. Perkins, <u>Agricultural Development in China</u>, pp. 92-98.

79. Ch'en Cheng-mo 陳正謨, <u>Chung-kuo ko-sheng ti ti-tsu</u>
中國各省的地租 [Land rents in China by province]
(Shanghai: Commercial Press, 1936), p. 43, found the incidence
of labor rents to be highest in Honan, Szechwan, Kweichow, and
Yunnan based on reports from 1,520 localities in twenty-two
provinces excluding Manchuria.

80. Directorate of Statistics, <u>Chung-hua min-kuo t'ung-chi t'i-yao, 1935</u>,
pp. 462-463, shows land values in Shantung in 1933 as roughly the
same as those in Chekiang; the NARB 1934 Shantung value, however,
is one-third lower than Chekiang.

81. In table 16(1) I have used Buck's alternative estimate derived from
his "Agricultural Survey" rather than his "Farm Survey" percen-
tages which are usually cited. The latter are obviously too low both
because his sample gives inadequate weight to the southern provinces,
and because the nature of the survey dictated that relatively acces-
sible localities dominated the data.

82. For regional variations in Kiangsu, see Ash, <u>Land Tenure in Pre-</u>
<u>Revolutionary China</u>, pp. 11-22; for Shantung and Hopei, Myers,
<u>The Chinese Economy</u>, pp. 234-240.

83. George Jamieson, "Tenure of Land in China and the Condition of
the Rural Population," <u>Journal of the North China Branch of the</u>
<u>Royal Asiatic Society</u>, 23 (1889): 59-117.

84. <u>Nung-ch'ing pao-kao</u>, 5.12 (December 1937): 330, in Chang,
<u>Agricultural History</u>, 3: 728-730.

85. Myers, <u>The Chinese Peasant Economy</u>, p. 223.

86. Amano, <u>Farm Economy</u>, 1: 299.

87.   Buck, <u>Land Utilization in China</u>, p. 333.

88.   National Government, Directorate of Statistics, <u>Chung-kuo tsu-tien</u>
      <u>chih-tu chih t'ung-chi fen-hsi</u> 中國租佃制度之統
      計分析 [Statistical analysis of China's land rent system]
      (Shanghai: Cheng-chung, 1946), p. 59.

89.   National Land Commission, <u>Ch'uan-kuo t'u-ti tiao-ch'a pao-kao kang-</u>
      <u>yao</u> 全國土地調查報告綱要 [Preliminary report
      of the national land survey] (Nanking, 1937), p. 46

90.   Ministry of the Interior, <u>Nei-cheng nien-chien</u> 內政年鑑
      [Yearbook of the Interior Ministry], 4 vols. (Shanghai: Commercial
      Press, 1936), 3, <u>t'u-ti</u>, chap. 12, (D) pp. 993-994. Ch'en Cheng-
      mo found <u>ya-tsu</u> widespread in 30 percent of reporting localities
      in 1933-1934 and present in 6 percent more. <u>Chung-kuo ko-sheng</u>
      <u>ti ti-tsu</u>, p. 61.

91.   <u>Ch'uan-kuo t'u-ti tiao-ch'a pao-kao kang-yao</u>, p. 44.

92.   <u>Chung-kuo tsu-tien chih-tu chih t'ung-chi fen-hsi</u>, p. 43. The data,
      comparing 1924 and 1934, show such small changes that they may
      not be significant at all.

93.   Buck, <u>Land Utilization in China</u>, p. 462; <u>Nung-ch'ing pao-kao</u>, 2.4
      (April 1934):30, in Yen, <u>Statistics</u>, p. 342; <u>Ch'uan-kuo t'u-ti tiao-</u>
      <u>ch'a pao-kao kang-yao</u>, p. 51.

94.   Buck, <u>Land Utilization in China</u>, p. 462: seventy-six percent of
      farm credit was for "non-productive purposes"; Amano, <u>Farm</u>
      <u>Economy</u>, 2:219-220, citing seven national and local studies.

95.   <u>Nung-ch'ing pao-kao</u>, 2.11 (November 1934):108-109, in <u>The</u>
      <u>Chinese Economic and Statistical Review</u>, 1.11 (November 1934):7.

96.   <u>The Chinese Economic and Statistical Review</u>, 1.11 (November
      1934):2.

97.   See Chang, <u>Agricultural History</u>, 3:206-214; Amano, <u>Farm</u>
      <u>Economy</u>, 2:308-348.

98.   Buck, <u>Land Utilization in China</u>, p. 233.

99.   See Chang, <u>Agricultural History</u>, 2:559-580; 3:9-65. Amano,
      <u>Farm Economy</u>, 2:1-158.

100. Myers, <u>The Chinese Peasant Economy</u>, pp. 278-287, briefly describes the damage and dislocations suffered by the north China rural economy during 1937-1948.

101. Central Ministry of Agriculture, Planning Office, <u>Liang-nien lai ti Chung-kuo nung-ts'un ching-chi tiao-ch'a hui-pien</u> 兩年來 的中國農村經濟調查彙編 [Collection of surveys of the rural economy of China during the past two years] (Shanghai: Chung-hua, 1952), pp. 141-144, 149-151, 160, 162, 226-236.

102. D. K. Lieu, <u>China's Industries and Finance</u> (Peking: Chinese Government Bureau of Economic Information, 1927), pp. 197-219; Ku Lang 顧琅, <u>Chung-kuo shih ta-k'uang tiao-ch'a chi</u> 中國 十大礦廠調查記 [Report of an investigation of the ten largest mines in China] (Shanghai, 1916), section 3, p. 49.

103. American Bankers Association, Commission on Commerce and Marine, <u>China, An Economic Survey, 1923</u> (New York, 1928) p. 16.

104. National Economic Council, Bureau of Public Roads, <u>Highways in China</u> (Nanking, 1935).

105. Yen, <u>Statistics</u>, pp. 172-180. Mileage estimates in other sources differ slightly.

106. Chang Kia-ngau, <u>China's Struggle for Railroad Development</u> (New York: John Day, 1943), table III, pp. 170-171.

107. Hou, <u>Foreign Investment and Economic Development in China</u>, pp. 32, 39-42.

108. Yen, <u>Statistics</u>, p. 210.

109. Chinese Ministry of Information, <u>China Handbook, 1937-1945</u> (New York: Macmillan, 1947), p. 217.

110. Mantetsu Chōsabu 滿鐵調查部 , <u>Chū-shi no minsengyō</u> 中支の民船業 [The junk trade of central China] (Tokyo: Hakubunkan, 1943), pp. 134-135.

111. Yang Tuan-liu 楊端六, et al., <u>Liu-shih-wu nien-lai Chung-kuo kuo-chi mao-i t'ung-chi</u> 六十五年來中國國際貿 易統計 [Statistics of China's foreign trade during the last

sixty-five years] (National Research Institute of Social Sciences, Academia Sinica, 1931), p. 140.

112. Yen, Statistics, pp. 228-229, 235-236.

113. Chia Shih-i 賈士毅 , Min-kuo ts'ai-cheng shih 民國財政史 [Fiscal history of the Republic], 2 vols. (Shanghai: Commercial Press, 1917), 1:45-77.

114. Stanley F. Wright, China's Customs Revenue since the Revolution of 1911, 3rd ed. (Shanghai: Inspectorate General of Customs, 1935), pp. 440-441.

115. P. T. Chen, "Public Finance," The Chinese Year Book, 1935-1936 (Shanghai: Commercial Press, 1935), pp. 1298-1299.

116. Ch'ien Chia-chü 千家駒 , Chiu Chung-kuo kung-chai shih tzu-liao, 1894-1949 舊中國公債史資料, 1894-1949 [Source materials on government bond issues in old China, 1894-1949] (Peking: Ts'ai-cheng ching-chi, 1955), pp. 366-369.

117. Chia Te-huai 賈德懷 , Min-kuo ts'ai-cheng chien shih 民國財政簡史 [A short fiscal history of the Republic] (Shanghai: Commercial Press, 1946), pp. 697-698; Kashiwai Kisao 柏井象雄 , Kindai Shina zaisei shi 近代支那財政史 [History of modern Chinese finance] (Kyōto: Kyōiku Tosho, 1942), pp. 63-64.

118. C. M. Chang, "Local Government Expenditure in China," Monthly Bulletin of Economic China, 7.6 (June 1934): 233-247.

119. C. F. Remer, Foreign Investments in China (New York: Macmillan, 1933), pp. 123-147; Hsü I-sheng 徐義生 , Chung-kuo chin-tai wai-chai shih t'ung-chi tzu-liao, 1853-1927 中國近代外債史統計資料, 1853-1927 [Statistical materials on foreign loans in modern China, 1853-1927] (Peking: Chung-hua, 1962), pp. 240-245.

120. Remer, Foreign Investments in China, p. 160.

121. Arthur N. Young, China's Nation-Building Effort, 1927-1937: The Financial and Economic Record (Stanford: Hoover Institution Press, 1971), provides a comprehensive account. Douglas S. Paauw, "Chinese Public Finance during the Nanking Government

122

Period" (Ph. D. dissertation, Harvard University, 1950); "Chinese
National Expenditure during the Nanking Period," Far Eastern
Quarterly, 12.1 (November 1952):3-26; and "The Kuomintang and
Economic Stagnation," Journal of Asian Studies, 16.2 (February
1957):213-220, are less sanguine than Young.

122. U.S. Bureau of the Census, Historical Statistics of the United
States, 1789-1945 (Washington, D.C., 1949), p. 12.

123. Shun-hsin Chou, The Chinese Inflation, 1937-1949 (New York:
Columbia University Press, 1963), pp. 64-65; Chang, The
Inflationary Spiral, pp. 140-144.

124. Arthur N. Young, China and the Helping Hand, 1937-1945 (Cambridge: Harvard University Press, 1963), pp. 440-442.

125. Ch'ien, Chiu Chung-kuo kung-chai shih tzu-liao, pp. 370-375;
Young, China's Nation-Building Effort, pp. 459-468.

126. Young, China's Nation-Building Effort, pp. 98, 509-510. Young,
financial adviser to the Ministry of Finance, 1929-1947, disagrees
strongly with the lower estimate of a 50 to 60 percent net return
which appears in Leonard G. Ting, "Chinese Modern Banks and
the Finance of Government and Industry," Nankai Social and Economic Quarterly, 8.3 (October 1935):591 and elsewhere and
originates with Chu Hsieh 朱偰 , Chung-kuo ts'ai-cheng wen-t'i
中國財政問題 [Problems of China's public finance]
(Shanghai: Commercial Press, 1934), pp. 231-232.

127. Young, China's Nation-Building Effort, pp. 98-99.

128. Frank M. Tamagna, Banking and Finance in China (New York:
Institute of Pacific Relations, 1942), pp. 121-196; Miyashita Tadao
宮下忠雄 , Shina ginkō seido ron 支那銀行制度
論 [A treatise on the Chinese banking system] (Tokyo: Ganshōdō,
1941), pp. 103-221; Tokunaga Kiyoyuki 德永清行 , Shina
chūō ginkō ron 支那中央銀行論 [A treatise on central
banking in China] (Tokyo: Yūhikaku, 1942), pp. 235-350; Andrea
Lee McElderry, Shanghai Old-Style Banks (Ch'ien-chuang), 1800-
1935 (Ann Arbor: University of Michigan Center for Chinese Studies,
Michigan Papers in Chinese Studies No. 25, 1976), pp. 131-185.

129. On wartime and postwar public finance and the inflation, see Chou,
The Chinese Inflation; Chang, The Inflationary Spiral; and Arthur N.

Young, China's Wartime Finance and Inflation, 1937-1945 (Cambridge: Harvard University Press, 1965).

130. Robert F. Dernberger, "The Role of the Foreigner in China's Economic Development," in China's Modern Economy in Historical Perspective, ed. Perkins, pp. 28-30.

131. C. F. Remer, Foreign Investments in China, pp. 170-171.

132. Hou, Foreign Investment and Economic Development in China, pp. 17-22.

133. Hou, Foreign Investment and Economic Development in China, pp. 138-141.

134. Dernberger, "The Role of the Foreigner in China's Economic Development," pp. 39-40.

135. Hou, Foreign Investment and Economic Development in China, p. 29.

136. See Albert Feuerwerker, The Foreign Establishment in China in the Early Twentieth Century (Ann Arbor: University of Michigan Center for Chinese Studies, Michigan Papers in Chinese Studies No. 29, 1976).

MICHIGAN PAPERS IN CHINESE STUDIES

No. 2. The Cultural Revolution: 1967 in Review, four essays by Michel Oksenberg, Carl Riskin, Robert Scalapino, and Ezra Vogel.

No. 3. Two Studies in Chinese Literature, by Li Chi and Dale Johnson.

No. 4. Early Communist China: Two Studies, by Ronald Suleski and Daniel Bays.

No. 5. The Chinese Economy, ca. 1870-1911, by Albert Feuerwerker,

No. 6. Chinese Paintings in Chinese Publications, 1956-1968: An Annotated Bibliography and an Index to the Paintings, by E. J. Laing.

No. 7. The Treaty Ports and China's Modernization: What Went Wrong? by Rhoads Murphey.

No. 8. Two Twelfth Century Texts on Chinese Painting, by Robert J. Maeda.

No. 9. The Economy of Communist China, 1949-1969, by Chu-yuan Cheng.

No. 10. Educated Youth and the Cultural Revolution in China, by Martin Singer.

No. 11. Premodern China: A Bibliographical Introduction, by Chun-shu Chang.

No. 12. Two Studies on Ming History, by Charles O. Hucker.

No. 13. Nineteenth Century China: Five Imperialist Perspectives, selected by Dilip Basu, edited by Rhoads Murphey.

No. 14. Modern China, 1840-1972: An Introduction to Sources and Research Aids, by Andrew J. Nathan.

No. 15. Women in China: Studies in Social Change and Feminism, edited by Marilyn B. Young.

No. 16. An Annotated Bibliography of Chinese Painting Catalogues and Related Texts, by Hin-cheung Lovell.

No. 17. China's Allocation of Fixed Capital Investment, 1952-1957, by Chu-yuan Cheng.

No. 18. Health, Conflict, and the Chinese Political System, by David M. Lampton.

No. 19. Chinese and Japanese Music-Dramas, edited by J. I. Crump and William P. Malm.

No. 20. Hsin-lun (New Treatise) and Other Writings by Huan T'an (43 B.C. – 28 A.D.), translated by Timoteus Pokora.

No. 21. Rebellion in Nineteenth-Century China, by Albert Feuerwerker.

No. 22. Between Two Plenums: China's Intraleadership Conflict, 1959-1962, by Ellis Joffe.

No. 23. "Proletarian Hegemony" in the Chinese Revolution and the Canton Commune of 1927, by S. Bernard Thomas.

No. 24. Chinese Communist Materials at the Bureau of Investigation Archives, Taiwan, by Peter Donovan, Carl E. Dorris, and Lawrence R. Sullivan.

No. 25. Shanghai Old-Style Banks (Ch'ien-chuang), 1800-1935, by Andrea Lee McElderry.

No. 26. The Sian Incident: A Pivotal Point in Modern Chinese History, by Tien-wei Wu.

No. 27. State and Society in Eighteenth-Century China: The Ch'ing Empire in Its Glory, by Albert Feuerwerker.

No. 28. Intellectual Ferment for Political Reforms in Taiwan, 1971-1973, by Mab Huang.

No. 29. The Foreign Establishment in China in the Early Twentieth Century, by Albert Feuerwerker.

No. 30. A Translation of Lao Tzu's "Tao Te Ching" and Wang Pi's "Commentary," by Paul J. Lin.

No. 31. Economic Trends in the Republic of China, 1912-1949, by Albert Feuerwerker.

MICHIGAN ABSTRACTS OF CHINESE AND
JAPANESE WORKS ON CHINESE HISTORY

No. 1. The Ming Tribute Grain System, by Hoshi Ayao, translated by Mark Elvin.

No. 2. Commerce and Society in Sung China, by Shiba Yoshinobu, translated by Mark Elvin.

No. 3. Transport in Transition: The Evolution of Traditional Shipping in China, translations by Andrew Watson.

No. 4. Japanese Perspectives on China's Early Modernization: A Bibliographical Survey, by K. H. Kim.

No. 5. The Silk Industry in Ch'ing China, by Shih Min-hsiung, translated by E-tu Zen Sun.

NONSERIES PUBLICATION

Index to the "Chan-kuo Ts'e," by Sharon Fidler and J. I. Crump. A companion volume to the Chan-kuo Ts'e, translated by J. I. Crump (Oxford: Clarendon Press, 1970).

Michigan Papers and Abstracts available from:

Center for Chinese Studies
The University of Michigan
Lane Hall (Publications)
Ann Arbor, MI 48109 USA

Prepaid Orders Only
write for complete price listing